Mindfulness

How Tapping Into Mindfulness Power in You Will Change Your Life

(Develop Self-awareness, Reduce Stress and Manage Negative Emction)

Douglas Henson

Published by Rob Miles

© **Douglas Henson**

All Rights Reserved

Mindfulness: How Tapping Into Mindfulness Power in You Will Change Your Life (Develop Self-awareness, Reduce Stress and Manage Negative Emotion)

ISBN 978-1-989990-84-1

All rights reserved. No part of this guide may be reproduced in any form without permission in writing from the publisher except in the case of brief quotations embodied in critical articles or reviews.

Legal & Disclaimer

The information contained in this book is not designed to replace or take the place of any form of medicine or professional medical advice. The information in this book has been provided for educational and entertainment purposes only.

The information contained in this book has been compiled from sources deemed reliable, and it is accurate to the best of the Author's knowledge; however, the Author cannot guarantee its accuracy and validity and cannot be held liable for any errors or omissions. Changes are periodically made to this book. You must consult your doctor or get professional medical advice before using any of the suggested remedies, techniques, or information in this book.

Upon using the information contained in this book, you agree to hold harmless the Author from and against any damages, costs, and expenses, including any legal fees potentially resulting from the application of any of the information provided by this guide. This disclaimer applies to any damages or injury caused by the use and application, whether directly or indirectly, of any advice or information presented, whether for breach of contract, tort, negligence, personal injury, criminal intent, or under any other cause of action.

You agree to accept all risks of using the information presented inside this book. You need to consult a professional medical practitioner in order to ensure you are both able and healthy enough to participate in this program.

Table of Contents

INTRODUCTION 1

CHAPTER 1: THE BENEFITS OF MINDFULNESS 5

CHAPTER 2: THE BENEFITS OF MINDFULNESS 15

CHAPTER 3: HOW TO ENTER A BEGINNERS MINDSET 21

CHAPTER 4: GETTING STARTED WITH MINDFULNESS 36

CHAPTER 5: GETTING STARTED WITH MINDFULNESS 54

CHAPTER 6: HISTORY OF MEDITATION 72

CHAPTER 7: COMMON MINDFULNESS MYTHS 80

CHAPTER 8: UNDERSTANDING YOUR CURRENT SITUATION 92

CHAPTER 9: BENEFITS 99

CHAPTER 10: YOGA MEDITATION 110

CHAPTER 11: HOW DOES MINDFULNESS HELP YOU? 115

CHAPTER 12: UNDERSTANDING PAST AND FUTURE 122

CHAPTER 13: UNDERSTANDING PAST AND FUTURE 134

CHAPTER 14: MINDFULNESS EXERCISES FOR BEGINNERS! 146

CHAPTER 15: THE THREE UNIVERSAL TRUTHS 153

CHAPTER 16: LIVING WITH INTENTION 160

CHAPTER 17: STOP BEATING YOURSELF UP 172

CHAPTER 18: SITTING MEDITATION	176
CHAPTER 19: WHAT IS MEDITATION?	187
CHAPTER 20: LETTING GO	193
CHAPTER 21: CONDITIONING + MINDFULNESS = CREATIVITY	196
CONCLUSION	198

Introduction

If you're like me, you have felt flustered and out of sorts at your job. Deadlines must be met. Team members depend on us to get our work done. And more often than not our bosses have unrealistic expectations of how much work can be done in our days.

I wrote this book to help people to better understand why they get stressed at work and, more importantly, to enable and empower them to minimize the effects of workplace stress.

Before we move on to the first chapter, I want to help you evaluate how stressed you are at your job. This is a short exercise that you can do on a scratchpad or in your journal. If you're sitting at your desk reading this on your Kindle, go ahead and do it right now. It won't take but a moment.

Make three columns on a piece of paper. Label the first column "Event". In this column make a short list of at least five, but no more than ten things that cause you to feel stressed at work. Be as specific as you can. Marking down "work" is too broad and general. The list can be in any order you like.

Put "How Stressful" in the header for the second column. Next to each event assign a number between one and ten to note how much stress you feel when this event happens. One is not very stressful at all. Ten is the most extreme stress.

Atop the third column write "Last Time This Happened". Fill out the column with the day and if you remember the time this stressful situation most recently occurred.

This will give you some baseline stressors that we will want to keep in mind as we practice and learn the mindfulness techniques within the book. Our goal is to change the highly stressful moments into ones where you can make better choices.

We do this through greater awareness of the moment. That's precisely what mindfulness is. As you become more aware of the situation, you are able to make better choices. I want to help you focus your attention to the present moment so you can then approach each situation that arises with openness, acceptance and peace.

In the pages ahead we'll look at some basics of mindfulness and learn the techniques that best alleviate workplace stress. This will lead to the creation of a five minute program that you can do every day at work. Finally, I'll share some advanced tips to keep your mind at peace and your environment free of clutter.

Thanks again for downloading this book. I hope you enjoy it!

Chapter 1: The Benefits Of Mindfulness

There are many benefits that come from being more mindful and practicing mindful meditation. Physically and mentally you will notice a dramatic difference in both the quality of your health and the quality of your life after you start making mindfulness a daily practice. Here is a quick look at some of the biggest benefits of this ancient practice for both physical and mental health.

Physical Health Benefits

One of the physical health benefits of mindfulness and mindful meditation is the reduction of chronic pain associated with conditions like Fibromyalgia. auto-immune diseases and chronic conditions like Chronic Fatigue Syndrome, Lupus, and

Fibromyalgia are thought to be triggered by things like anxiety and stress.

Recent research indicates that the pain associated with Fibromyalgia is a physical reaction to the anxiety and tension that someone feels. Practicing mindful meditation or just taking a few minutes to put yourself in a mindful state can reduce or even eliminate the chronic pain associated with these conditions. By controlling the anxiety that they are feeling people who suffer from these conditions can stop the muscle tightening and other physical actions that contribute to chronic pain.

Stress Reduction

Stress and anxiety are responsible for a huge range of health problems that impact millions of people. The demands of modern life create so much stress that many people develop illnesses like:

Heart disease

High blood pressure

Obesity

Asthma

Diabetes

Fibromyalgia

Chronic Fatigue Syndrome

Migraines

Gastro-Intestinal illness

Insomnia

Cancer

Accelerated ageing

Alzheimer's

Mindful meditation and learning how to be present can lower the risk of disease caused by stress by up to 50% or more in some cases. Just a few minutes of mindful meditation each day can eliminate the physical effects of stress on the body. When you think about how much mindful meditation can do to keep you healthy you can see that it's totally worth it to start being more mindful in your everyday life.

The Mental Benefits

The mental benefits of mindfulness can be just as big as the physical ones. Just some of the incredible benefits that mindfulness and mindful mediation have mentally include:

Eliminating fear and anxiety

Managing the symptoms of depression

Better cognitive function

Improved memory

Better self-control

More self-insight

Better focus

More empathy

More compassion

More patience

Less irritability

Several studies that have been done have shown that developing more mindfulness can help people who suffer from anxiety disorders and depression and can make it possible for those who are at risk for depression and anxiety to manage their symptoms on their own, giving them control over their lives.

The Healing Power of Mindfulness

Mindfulness also has the power to help heal the wounds of people that suffer from PTSD, depression, anxiety and trauma. When people who have been through difficult situations, sometimes life-threatening situations, encounter triggers that cause them to panic or feel anxiety taking the time to breathe and look at the situation mindfully can help them stay present in the moment and not relive their trauma.

Mindfulness connects you to your body and emotions instead of distancing you from them. When you are battling a panic disorder or a traumatic memory, mindfulness can not only ground you in the present moment, it can also help you focus on something other than the trauma that you experienced.

Mindful Healing from Injuries or Illness

When a person is diagnosed with a serious illness or becomes injured, they can become mired in destructive thought patterns where they are constantly thinking about crisis and loss. For many people the first thoughts after an injury or an illness diagnose aren't about getting better, they are thoughts about the worst case scenario. Many people don't immediately focus on recovery or the impact of the illness or injury on themselves. Instead they start asking themselves like:

Those are all questions that people ask themselves in the wake of a big change in their lives. Mindfulness allows them to focus not on the negative impact of the injury or illness but on healing. The more focused they are on healing the easier it will be for them to heal.

Mindfulness means accepting the present situation without judgment or guilt. So instead of blaming or feeling guilty someone who is approaching a situation like this mindfully is focused on living well and healing. That kind of positive mental attitude is critically important to healing and developing the skills necessary to have a productive life after a catastrophic injury or illness.

It is difficult after a life changing event to let go of the past and focus on who you are now and what options lie in front of you but it's worth the effort to explore your new situation with mindfulness and an open heart. That way you can see the many different paths before you and not only see the path that is now behind you.

Some research has suggested that mindfulness can reduce chronic pain by up to 90%, although studies are ongoing. People who live with chronic pain that have learned how to live mindfully say that their pain is noticeably less now that they have adopted a more mindful lifestyle.

There are several components to using mindfulness to heal from injuries or illnesses. Mindful meditation, as well as gratitude and other practices, all combine to create a more mindful life. Accepting the present, including the pain and illness, gives people a sense of safety and allows them to begin rebuilding their lives as they are now, not as they were in the past.

Accepting your new reality is key to the process of moving on, and mindfulness can help with that acceptance. You may have to face that you have limitations that you have not had to deal with before but that also means you have new skills to balance out those limitations. When you strive for balance in your life and stay open to new ideas and practices you will be able to move forward even after a serious illness or injury.

Chapter 2: The Benefits Of Mindfulness

Everyone says mindfulness is beneficiary - but how exactly? Let's find out some of the ways that specific mindfulness exercises can help in the regular struggles and problems that we face every day.

It Changes Your Attitude and How You See Life!

Acquiring mindfulness helps you change your attitude and therefore your approach to life. When you are in the present you connect to the moment and savor every pleasure that it has to offer. You accept things as they are using all your senses. Increasing acceptance and using your every sense means you have better cognitive activity and you are capable of fully engaging in all activities.

The most significant that mindfulness has on a person is it adds to your level of acceptance and helps the acceptance of the adverse experiences with less worries and with less pain. It creates a certain level of dispassion towards life and greater capacity to handle negative situations. Being right here means you don't get caught up in regrets for the past or worry for the future. Life is no more a rat race cocooned in battle for success and glory, rather life becomes an opportunity, a gift and an adventure to explore.

It Helps Breathe Away Pain!

We are all in pain a lot of times in our lives, suffering from minor ailments such as migraine and cramps to bigger physical tragedies. Have you ever stopped to think, when in physical or emotional pain, how it completely takes over all our other senses, our emotions, and dominate our whole being?

With some specific mindfulness meditation exercises, it is possible to control our bodies' natural response to pain, and therefore, ease and alleviate our sufferings - not completely, but to a great extent. This is a great escape for people who suffer regularly from various chronic pains and discomforts.

It Drastically Improves Your Physical Health!

Mindfulness may be a mental exercise, but in recent times, scientists have discovered its many effects on a person's physical health too, including:

☐ Relieving stress

☐ Lowering blood pressure

☐ Improving Sleep

- Treat multiple heart diseases
- Reduce Chronic pains and
- Alleviate gastrointestinal problems

Mindfulness exercise, as we can see from the list above, almost has the same advantages to a human being as regular physical exercise and a healthy diet, thus making it an important part of our overall wellbeing.

It also Improves Mental Health!

Of course, mindfulness improves many aspects of our mental health too, as is the main focus of these exercises. These exercises show significant help in curing depression and conflicts among couples and families. They have also proven to have helped in many cases of eating disorder, substance abuse disorder, anxiety as well as obsessive-compulsive disorder in many people where other treatments have failed.

It keeps you Focused and Alert!

The main idea behind mindfulness exercises is to bring focus into wherever you are and whatever you are doing. It increases your mind's capacity to gain more information and to fully acknowledge any activity that you are engaged in, whether it is an important project that you are working on for your career, or reading a book at leisure.

People who practice mindfulness exercise know how to live in the moment and think about nothing else but the situation at hand. They don't spend every moment of their life worrying about the future, or contemplating on the past. Instead, they savor each and every moment they are living, and thus know how to enjoy life.

Practicing mindfulness exercises are a lifestyle choice, a way of living rather than something to try once or twice in a week. If you want to learn the techniques and exercises, you will also need to be prepared to go wholeheartedly in this practice, and not just as a one-time option to try and discard.

If you feel like you are ready to do so, the next chapter of our book will show you some of the proven and the most effective mindfulness exercise routines to follow.

Good luck!

Chapter 3: How To Enter A Beginners

Mindset

In the previous chapter we learned about stress, how it can be caused and the effect it can have on you mentally and physically. We even discussed several ways on how to manage your stress levels and maintain a healthier lifestyle. But what about your mind as a whole? How can you achieve that inner Zen that so many seem to have found? You can start with learning about Mindfulness.

In Zen Buddhism, there is a concept called shoshin, which translated means "beginner's mind." Shoshin is based on the premise that you can let go of your preconceived ideas and have an attitude of openness to new concepts. With the practice of Mindfulness gaining popularity among not only those who practice meditation but also among the psychotherapy community, it is easy to learn more about the practice and how to progress. Some of the benefits you can learn from the practice of mindfulness are learning self-control, tolerance, enhanced flexibility of mind, equanimity, and objectivity.

So what is Mindfulness and its practices? Mindfulness is the ability to be present and fully aware of what you are doing and where you are, while not being overwhelmed or overly reactive by what is going on around you. This means that your mind is completely aware of what is happening, what you are doing, and the space that you move through. Mindfulness helps you to respond reflectively to a situation rather than reacting to them because of habits you have been conditioned to. Mindfulness uses the experiences of the moment, including sounds, sensations in the body, smells, tastes, and breathing, as a way to anchor nonjudgmental attention, stabilizing your way of relating to your inner and outer experiences.

Mindfulness is not special. It is not added. The power to be in the present is already born within us. You just need to learn how to harness it. There are simple practices one can learn that have been scientifically proven to benefit yourself, those you love, friends, and coworkers. There is no need to change for mindfulness either. When an answer to a problem presents itself in the form of changing yourself, it typically fails. Change is hard. Mindfulness acknowledges this and brings out the best of who you are as a person.

Meditation is not something that is only in your head. It does not mean dwelling on your thoughts either. Meditation is based on your body. It requires you taking the time to listen to where you are and what you are doing, which generally starts with being aware of your body. This act can be very calming as you get in tune with your body's rhythms.

Mindfulness and Awareness

Mindfulness and Awareness go hand in hand. Mindfulness requires you to relate to your current situation definitely, directly, and precisely. The way you deal with irritating or frustrating situations usually involves emotions like aggression, restlessness, passion, and ignorance. These feelings are normal in today's world. They do not need to be shunned, you can consider them more like fits, such as a toddler would have, only this is your body reacting. You have been conditioned to react these ways, however, depending on your situation, they could be the precise reaction needed for that moment's frustrations. Being in a mindful state is just another way to clearly show what is there in front of you. This means that you are only aware of your active mind, which can be involved in several perceptions. The mind does not deal with the past or the future, it simply lives in the now. It is necessary when beginning to be aware of these dual perceptions because it helps you to refrain from making quick judgments.

Awareness, however, is being able to see the breakthrough of mindfulness. Through awareness, you can leave what is in your mind be, instead of tossing it away like yesterdays garbage. Mindfulness has its own location and space within the brain. Because of this awareness, you can take one more step to being able not to choose in a situation, or being "choiceless." This simply means that you react without judging, you recognize that it is what it is. Recognizing, or "recognition," the outcomes mindfulness can give you, such as recognizing passions, aggressions, frustrations, sadness, happiness, and joys, is also a large part of awareness. Another way of explaining this is by asking yourself "What should I do with this feeling I am experiencing right now?" or "What can I do next about this?" Having awareness then helps us to see that we do not necessarily need to do anything really, but can leave it to be in its own place within your mind.

Consider this example: You notice a beautiful flower while on a hike. Do you pick it and take it home with you? Or do you allow the flower to stay there in its natural environment? Awareness tells you to leave the flower alone because it is where it is meant to be. This means that awareness is the ability to be willing to not hang on to discoveries made by being mindful. Mindfulness is an act of being able to recognize that things are what they are. Because of this, mindfulness and awareness work together as a way to help you find acceptance in situations as they arise.

The practice of meditation is how you can diffuse yourself of stress. The amount of meditation you do often depend on the amount of stress that you are under. There are several ways to begin meditation, and a lot of it has to do with your physical locations, how you sit, breathe, and the environment around you. We will go into meditation and some exercises in depth in a later chapter, however, here are a few specific things you can do now to alleviate some of the anxieties and stress you may be experiencing, or encounter in the future.

Beginning Your Meditation

How you sit can play a large part in the process of meditation. Your posture too is important when you meditate. Just sitting quietly can be a wonderful way to relax, if even for a moment, before going back to your crazy routine.

This next exercise is a quick, easy way to practice meditation wherever you are. Find a seat that is comfortable for you depending on your physical needs and location. This could be a chair, the floor, or a bench. But it should be solid. Be aware of where your legs are at. If on the floor, cross them. If in a chair or bench, have both feet touching the ground. Keep your back and upper body straight, allowing the natural curve of your spine to remain. Keep your arms to the side of your body, placing hands on top of your legs.

Next, let you gaze drop and allow your head to tilt forward just a little. Closing your eyes is often practiced, but it is not necessary. Now that you have found the proper stance for meditation, stay there a few moments. Relax and allow yourself to just focus on you at that moment. Once you have found that calmness that comes from focusing inward, you can return to your day. If you begin to feel the pains of stress again, repeat the whole thing.

This is a quick a simple way of practicing mindfulness daily, and easy for the beginner. This is all that it is, combined with some breathing techniques that we will discuss in a moment. Remembering to do this several times a day, or when you feel your blood pressure start to rise because the stress is getting to you is the hard part. As you continue to practice this, you will notice that your results will gradually grow.

Remember from the previous chapter, that stress triggers a specific response within our bodies, bringing out the primitive nature of the brain, that fight or flight response. Only after you have dealt with the current trigger will your body return to its normal state. You can get back to your normal state by practicing the mindfulness techniques at that moment, and reduce them altogether by frequent practicing.

Good times to practice these meditations are throughout your day, simply by shifting your mind away from the moment and taking a few deep breaths, or just a brief pause. Sometimes you may want to consider taking these moments could include:

When you wake up in the morning or before bed

Going to the bathroom

While waiting for your computer to load

Before answering the phone or replying to a text message

Before and after meetings

And especially before speaking during a stressful conversation

The next step is to not only continue to practice these quick moments of mindfulness and awareness but adding breathing to the equation. As with all types of fitness, mental fitness comes with training. So practice daily, and soon you will see the benefits begin to take hold.

Here is a simple 5-minute breathing technique you can incorporate into a mindful state of meditation. This can be done daily, or multiple times a day.

Place yourself in a comfortable position, either practicing the sitting technique discussed earlier or laying down.

Close your eyes if you choose. If not, allow your gaze to become unfocused, not fixating on an object.

Turn your thoughts inward to your present moment by paying attention to what you are feeling physically. You can do this by checking your body from head to toe. Tell yourself to let any tension located in your body to go away.

Once you have let all tension release, focus on how you are breathing. Notice your breath going in and out. Next, when you breathe, pay attention to your chest as it rises and falls. Then focus on your stomach as it rises and falls with each breath.

Choose a vantage point to focus on, then pay attention to the breaths as they come and go. Make sure to follow the breath from start to finish, fully inhaling naturally and exhaling naturally, some may be short, long, deep, or shallow.

If your mind wanders while focusing on each breath, which is very common, pay attention to where it wanders off to, then bring yourself back to the task at hand of felling how you are breathing and each breath going in and out.

It is natural for the mind to wander during these sessions. Do not let this discourage you. All you need to do is to catch yourself and gently bring yourself back to the breathing exercise.

Last, do this daily, at least for one week. At the end of the week see how you are feeling about allowing yourself time to be within yourself and allowing your body the ability to detach and therefore de-clutter.

By practicing mindful breathing, you are strengthening a muscle that helps you live in the present. The more you practice, the more you will discover how easy it will be to stay in the present, instead of getting trapped into the past or some daydream about the future. Living in the now will help you to feel more at peace and with more clarity, thus helping you to deal with difficult circumstances. Mindfulness is not a reason to tune out the world, but it is about tuning in, with more compassion and open awareness. As you being to relate to life from this vantage point, you will discover a whole new world of opportunities.

A few things to remember about having a Beginner's Mind:

Take one step at a time

If you fall several times, get up several more times

Do not pre-judge. Instead, think of it as I do not know mine

Do not live with an "I should have" attitude

Do not make experiences negative, instead use experience, keeping an open mind which will allow you to apply mindfulness to a new circumstance.

Stop being the expert.

Forget common sense

Do not let fear of failure guide you

Focus on the questions and not the answers.

As you develop your Beginner's mind, you learn to become much more open to new possibilities and more creative. You will forge new friendships with others as they begin to notice your interest in them and your appreciation for their ideas and thoughts on things. This is what Beginner's Mind is all about. We have covered the basis of Beginner's Mind and some basic meditation and breathing techniques to help start your journey down this path. Let us now consider how Beginner's Mind can help you in other aspects of your life, such as how to be non-judgmental, how to deal with greed, delusions, acceptance and letting go.

Chapter 4: Getting Started With

Mindfulness

Practicing mindfulness meditation involves maintaining attention on one or combination of the following:

Breath

Senses

Thoughts or emotions

Mindfulness can be practiced as a formal meditation or informal meditation. Formal mindfulness meditation is practiced sitting in a quiet environment with eyes closed. Formal meditation is more effective than any other mindfulness practice.

Informal mindfulness meditation can be practiced at any time throughout the day. There are two types of informal meditation— micro-hits and background.

Micro-hits meditation can be practiced anywhere and the duration of practice ranges from a few seconds to five minutes. Background meditation is about going into a meditation state of mind while doing a task. This can be anything from listening to music, driving a car, to doing household chores. In this chapter, we will learn how to practice formal mindfulness meditation.

Preparing the Environment

Practicing mindfulness meditation requires a quiet place, a comfortable way to sit and a few minutes of time to focus on something besides your usual planning. A quiet environment helps the beginners to maintain the focus. If the environment is not perfectly quiet, that's fine. We can use noise and distraction as a part of our meditation.

Turn your phone off or set it to silent mode and get rid of other distractions if possible. Wear loose fitting and comfortable clothing.

Posture is essential for mindfulness meditation. Serious practitioners emphasize the benefit of firm postures. If you are a yoga practitioner, you can practice in a full-lotus or half-lotus position. You can also practice sitting on a chair, on the couch or on the floor. If you're sitting on the chair, keep your legs uncrossed with your feet touching the floor.

Sit comfortably in the relaxed postures with back straight (not stiff). You can also practice in lying position, but most people feel sleepy in the lying posture. That's why it is not recommended unless you have conditions like back pain or other illnesses. Whatever postures you choose for your practice, make sure that you feel comfortable in that position.

Try to meditate in the same place at the same time every day. You can turn on some gentle music if you like. It is important to feel joy and happiness while practicing mindfulness. So meditate with a little smile on your face.

Set a specific time for your mindfulness practice. Don't practice meditation when you are in a hurry. If you're unsure about when to end your meditation, you can use a clock. Practicing 10 minutes every day should be enough for the beginner level. Don't try too hard or lengthen your meditation too quickly— that can slow your progress. Slight movement is ok during practice. While practicing mindfulness, if you find yourself caught up in a struggle between the desire to move and the intention not to, feel free to move if you have to. But become mindful and aware of the moment. We are going to start our practice with breath awareness.

The Practice of Meditation

Mindfulness of Breath

Breath awareness is the easiest way to start your mindfulness program. Breath is always with us, and our mind can always come back to breath as an object of attention. Respiration is a spontaneous process— no one teaches us to breathe, nor do we need any skill to focus on the process of breathing.

Breathing provides the supply of oxygen that keeps every organ of our body functional. In Sanskrit breath is called "Prana" or the life force.

While maintaining your attention on the breath during meditation, keep in mind that you can't control your breathing— the process of breathing has to be spontaneous.

Meditation is not a breathing exercise. To practice mindfulness meditation, sit down in a relaxed posture. Close your eyes and take a few moments to gather your attention by simply being fully present with your breath as it enters and leaves your body.

Normal breathing is slow, effortless and fluid. Pay your attention to this spontaneous movement of your breathing cycle. Escort your awareness to the place in your body where you clearly experience the process of breathing. It may be your nostrils where you feel the inflow and the outflow. Notice when the air enters into your nostrils, you feel cool. When the air moves out of your nostrils, you feel warm. Stay with the movement of air, with the feeling of warmth or coolness.

You may also rest your attention on your chest or abdomen. Observe the expansion and contraction of your chest with each inhalation and each exhalation or the rise and fall of your belly with the inflow and the outflow of your breath.

Now focus on the sensation of air moving in and out of your body as you breathe in or breathe out. Pay attention to the way each breath changes.

Your mind will often drift from your breath. When it happens, remind yourself to re-connect with the natural rhythm—and gently drift back. Maintain your attention on your breath.

Breathe effortlessly and remain present throughout the whole sequence of inhaling, exhaling and pausing between breaths. Pay attention and relax into each breath. Don't let the process of paying attention affect the natural rhythm of your breathing. Sustain your attention throughout the entire breath-cycle— one breath at a time.

Stay with your breath from the moment it rises in your awareness until the next breath begins. Use your breath as an anchor for your attention— return to your breath every time your mind moves away.

Your respiratory rhythm will change automatically. Sometimes your breath will be long, sometimes short, and sometimes shallow. Be aware of the change and allow it to be the way it is.

Thoughts will bubble up. Every time you get carried away in your thoughts, notice where your mind went off to, then gently return to your breath.

Beginners may find it a bit hard to maintain their attention for more than a few minutes. But with regular practice, their attention span will increase. After a week or two, increase the duration of your practice by ten minutes. You can increase the duration by up to half an hour or longer, if you feel comfortable. But avoid trying hard or lengthening your meditation too quickly.

Mindfulness of Sound

Sound awareness is the second step of your mindfulness meditation. After practicing mindfulness of breath for a week, expand your field of awareness so that it includes sound.

To practice mindfulness of sound, start with maintaining your attention on your breath, as in the preceding exercise. After a couple of minutes, shift your awareness from breath to sounds as they spontaneously call your attention to them and away from your breath. Be conscious of the sounds inside or outside the room—

the sound of clock ticking, wind blowing, peoples' chattering, distant traffic, car horns, or other noises…whatever the sound is, simply pay effortless attention to it without thinking about the source— notice as it rises and falls in this open field of awareness.

There are spaces between sounds. The space is silence. Focus on the silence.

Now pay closer attention to the subtle sounds. You don't have to look for a particular sound. Just expand your awareness to become present of the sounds all around you. Become aware of the sounds as they arise from all directions— obvious sounds, distant sounds, sounds that are in front, behind, to the side, above or below. Direct your attention to various sounds that present themselves to you. Become aware of the sounds spontaneously. You don't need to think about the source.

The moment you find yourself thinking about the sound, reconnect as best as you can. Instead of focusing on the meaning or implication of sounds, move your attention to their sensory characteristics, such as loudness, pitch, timbre, and frequency. Now become aware of your reaction to sounds. Notice whether the mind has identified the sound as pleasant or unpleasant. Observe your reaction without clinging to them or resisting them. Whenever the thought arises, and you find your mind drifted away, calmly move your attention back to the sounds as they rise and fall from one moment to the next.

After practicing sound awareness for a while, the sound will no longer attract your attention. If boredom creeps in, return to your primary object of awareness— your breath.

Mindfulness of Sensations

After practicing sound awareness for a few days, expand your awareness to include bodily sensations. Direct your attention to any sensation that you notice in your entire body. Move your focus to the quality of the sensation.

Is it a feeling of tension or numbness? Whatever it is, be present with that sensation. Notice what happens as you focus your attention on that sensation. See how accurately you can recognize each sensation as it enters into your awareness. Observe your reactions to the sensations— any clinging or avoidance or other reactions.

Avoid judging your sensations. Simply notice as they appear, peak, and disappear. See if your attention amplifies the sensation or weaken it or make it disappear. Don't attempt to change the way you feel. Just stay with the sensation

Sensations are transient in nature. They will fade away on their own.

After a while, the sensations no longer hold your attention. Shift your attention back to your breath.

Mindfulness of Emotions

In this stage of mindfulness meditation, we will include awareness of emotion in our practice. Emotions will inevitably arise in your consciousness.

As soon as an emotion surfaces into your awareness, identify it and accept it nonjudgmentally.

Stay in a receptive mood as you become aware of your emotional state. Remain open and permit yourself to be completely present with the emotion. Direct all your attention to fully experience the emotion.

Our mind registers an emotion as pleasant or unpleasant or neutral. If the emotion is pleasant, the mind clings to it, if it is unpleasant, the mind tends to push it away. But when mindfulness takes place, the mind accepts emotions just the way they are, without judging. Whenever the emotion appears in your consciousness, simply allow it to remain in your awareness without pursuing it.

Strong emotions can be a little tricky to navigate. When a strong emotion arises, be open to a mindful inquiry, reflect on the nature of the emotion itself, without becoming involved in the story behind it. Mark the emotion with a mental note. For instance, if you feel irritated, you can level it "anger", if you feel sad, label the emotion as "grief" or "sadness". Allow yourself to fully experience the emotion. Learn to face it.

Being mindful of the emotion will change your relationship with that particular emotion. If you can become mindful of stress, you no longer have to resist it. You'll only accept it with a non-reactive awareness.

Choice-less Awareness

This is an advanced stage of awareness, where anything arises in the background of your consciousness, whether it is sound, thoughts, images, sensation or emotion, you'll allow it to remain there, focusing primarily on the flow of your breathing. If a sound predominates the background of your awareness, make it a focus of your attention. If a thought, image or sensation predominates the background, make it your object of focus and expand your field of awareness to include the entire range of experience— breath, sounds, thoughts, images, sensations, and emotions.

Fully experience anything that arises into your consciousness, letting your mind settle without wavering, wherever it goes.

Ending Your Practice

Ending your meditation session is as important as the meditation itself. A thoughtless transition from meditation to ordinary consciousness may generate discomforts like irritability, stress or headaches. Therefore it is important to take care when you end your meditation— coming out too quickly can ruin a perfectly good meditation. When its time to end your meditation, be aware that you're going to end your meditation soon. Your body will immediately shift gears from a meditative mood to neutral gear.

Don't hurry out of your practice. Take a minute to transition gradually after meditation before opening your eyes or standing up.

Shift your focus from inward to outward. Be conscious of your surrounding.

Open your eyes a little, then close. Open your eyes again— a little more. Stay seated for half a minute. Now move your upper body slowly and gently— head, neck, shoulders... do a seated spinal twist of some kind. Stretch your arms.

Move your lower body— start with your toes. Then gently move your feet, ankles, and legs. Now stand up.

A good closing ritual helps you to absorb the full benefit of your practice.

Chapter 5: Getting Started With Mindfulness

Practicing mindfulness meditation involves maintaining attention on one or combination of the following:

Breath

Senses

Thoughts or emotions

Mindfulness can be practiced as a formal meditation or informal meditation. Formal mindfulness meditation is practiced sitting in a quiet environment with eyes closed. Formal meditation is more effective than any other mindfulness practice.

Informal mindfulness meditation can be practiced at any time throughout the day. There are two types of informal meditation— micro-hits and background. Micro-hits meditation can be practiced anywhere and the duration of practice ranges from a few seconds to five minutes. Background meditation is about going into a meditation state of mind while doing a task. This can be anything from listening to music, driving a car, to doing household chores. In this chapter, we will learn how to practice formal mindfulness meditation.

Preparing the Environment

Practicing mindfulness meditation requires a quiet place, a comfortable way to sit and a few minutes of time to focus on something besides your usual planning. A quiet environment helps the beginners to maintain the focus. If the environment is not perfectly quiet, that's fine. We can use noise and distraction as a part of our meditation.

Turn your phone off or set it to silent mode and get rid of other distractions if possible. Wear loose fitting and comfortable clothing.

Posture is essential for mindfulness meditation. Serious practitioners emphasize the benefit of firm postures. If you are a yoga practitioner, you can practice in a full-lotus or half-lotus position. You can also practice sitting on a chair, on the couch or on the floor. If you're sitting on the chair, keep your legs uncrossed with your feet touching the floor.

Sit comfortably in the relaxed postures with back straight (not stiff). You can also practice in lying position, but most people feel sleepy in the lying posture. That's why it is not recommended unless you have conditions like back pain or other illnesses. Whatever postures you choose for your practice, make sure that you feel comfortable in that position.

Try to meditate in the same place at the same time every day. You can turn on some gentle music if you like. It is important to feel joy and happiness while practicing mindfulness. So meditate with a little smile on your face.

Set a specific time for your mindfulness practice. Don't practice meditation when you are in a hurry. If you're unsure about when to end your meditation, you can use a clock. Practicing 10 minutes every day should be enough for the beginner level. Don't try too hard or lengthen your meditation too quickly— that can slow your progress. Slight movement is ok during practice. While practicing mindfulness, if you find yourself caught up in a struggle between the desire to move and the intention not to, feel free to move if you have to. But become mindful and aware of the moment. We are going to start our practice with breath awareness.

The Practice of Meditation

Mindfulness of Breath

Breath awareness is the easiest way to start your mindfulness program. Breath is always with us, and our mind can always come back to breath as an object of attention. Respiration is a spontaneous process— no one teaches us to breathe, nor do we need any skill to focus on the process of breathing.

Breathing provides the supply of oxygen that keeps every organ of our body functional. In Sanskrit breath is called "Prana" or the life force.

While maintaining your attention on the breath during meditation, keep in mind that you can't control your breathing—the process of breathing has to be spontaneous.

Meditation is not a breathing exercise. To practice mindfulness meditation, sit down in a relaxed posture. Close your eyes and take a few moments to gather your attention by simply being fully present with your breath as it enters and leaves your body.

Normal breathing is slow, effortless and fluid. Pay your attention to this spontaneous movement of your breathing cycle. Escort your awareness to the place in your body where you clearly experience the process of breathing. It may be your nostrils where you feel the inflow and the outflow. Notice when the air enters into your nostrils, you feel cool. When the air moves out of your nostrils, you feel warm. Stay with the movement of air, with the feeling of warmth or coolness.

You may also rest your attention on your chest or abdomen. Observe the expansion and contraction of your chest with each inhalation and each exhalation or the rise and fall of your belly with the inflow and the outflow of your breath.

Now focus on the sensation of air moving in and out of your body as you breathe in or breathe out. Pay attention to the way each breath changes.

Your mind will often drift from your breath. When it happens, remind yourself to re-connect with the natural rhythm— and gently drift back. Maintain your attention on your breath.

Breathe effortlessly and remain present throughout the whole sequence of inhaling, exhaling and pausing between breaths. Pay attention and relax into each breath. Don't let the process of paying attention affect the natural rhythm of your breathing. Sustain your attention throughout the entire breath-cycle— one breath at a time.

Stay with your breath from the moment it rises in your awareness until the next breath begins. Use your breath as an anchor for your attention— return to your breath every time your mind moves away.

Your respiratory rhythm will change automatically. Sometimes your breath will be long, sometimes short, and sometimes shallow. Be aware of the change and allow it to be the way it is.

Thoughts will bubble up. Every time you get carried away in your thoughts, notice where your mind went off to, then gently return to your breath.

Beginners may find it a bit hard to maintain their attention for more than a few minutes. But with regular practice, their attention span will increase. After a week or two, increase the duration of your practice by ten minutes. You can increase the duration by up to half an hour or longer, if you feel comfortable. But avoid trying hard or lengthening your meditation too quickly.

Mindfulness of Sound

Sound awareness is the second step of your mindfulness meditation. After practicing mindfulness of breath for a week, expand your field of awareness so that it includes sound.

To practice mindfulness of sound, start with maintaining your attention on your breath, as in the preceding exercise. After a couple of minutes, shift your awareness from breath to sounds as they spontaneously call your attention to them and away from your breath. Be conscious of the sounds inside or outside the room— the sound of clock ticking, wind blowing, peoples' chattering, distant traffic, car horns, or other noises...whatever the sound is, simply pay effortless attention to it without thinking about the source— notice as it rises and falls in this open field of awareness.

There are spaces between sounds. The space is silence. Focus on the silence.

Now pay closer attention to the subtle sounds. You don't have to look for a particular sound. Just expand your awareness to become present of the sounds all around you. Become aware of the sounds as they arise from all directions— obvious sounds, distant sounds, sounds that are in front, behind, to the side, above or below. Direct your attention to various sounds that present themselves to you. Become aware of the sounds spontaneously. You don't need to think about the source.

The moment you find yourself thinking about the sound, reconnect as best as you can. Instead of focusing on the meaning or implication of sounds, move your attention to their sensory characteristics, such as loudness, pitch, timbre, and frequency. Now become aware of your reaction to sounds. Notice whether the mind has identified the sound as pleasant or unpleasant. Observe your reaction without clinging to them or resisting them. Whenever the thought arises, and you find your mind drifted away, calmly move your attention back to the sounds as they rise and fall from one moment to the next.

After practicing sound awareness for a while, the sound will no longer attract your attention. If boredom creeps in, return to your primary object of awareness— your breath.

Mindfulness of Sensations

After practicing sound awareness for a few days, expand your awareness to include bodily sensations. Direct your attention to any sensation that you notice in your entire body. Move your focus to the quality of the sensation.

Is it a feeling of tension or numbness? Whatever it is, be present with that sensation. Notice what happens as you focus your attention on that sensation. See how accurately you can recognize each sensation as it enters into your awareness. Observe your reactions to the sensations— any clinging or avoidance or other reactions.

Avoid judging your sensations. Simply notice as they appear, peak, and disappear. See if your attention amplifies the sensation or weaken it or make it disappear. Don't attempt to change the way you feel. Just stay with the sensation

Sensations are transient in nature. They will fade away on their own.

After a while, the sensations no longer hold your attention. Shift your attention back to your breath.

Mindfulness of Emotions

In this stage of mindfulness meditation, we will inc ude awareness of emotion in our practice. Emotions will inevitably arise in your consciousness.

As soon as an emotion surfaces into your awareness, identify it and accept it nonjudgmentally.

Stay in a receptive mood as you become aware of your emotional state. Remain open and permit yourself to be completely present with the emotion. Direct all your attention to fully experience the emotion.

Our mind registers an emotion as pleasant or unpleasant or neutral. If the emotion is pleasant, the mind clings to it, if it is unpleasant, the mind tends to push it away. But when mindfulness takes place, the mind accepts emotions just the way they are, without judging. Whenever the emotion appears in your consciousness, simply allow it to remain in your awareness without pursuing it.

Strong emotions can be a little tricky to navigate. When a strong emotion arises, be open to a mindful inquiry, reflect on the nature of the emotion itself, without becoming involved in the story behind it. Mark the emotion with a mental note. For instance, if you feel irritated, you can level it "anger", if you feel sad, label the emotion as "grief" or "sadness". Allow yourself to fully experience the emotion. Learn to face it.

Being mindful of the emotion will change your relationship with that particular emotion. If you can become mindful of stress, you no longer have to resist it. You'll only accept it with a non-reactive awareness.

Choice-less Awareness

This is an advanced stage of awareness, where anything arises in the background of your consciousness, whether it is sound, thoughts, images, sensation or emotion, you'll allow it to remain there, focusing primarily on the flow of your breathing. If a sound predominates the background of your awareness, make it a focus of your attention. If a thought, image or sensation predominates the background, make it your object of focus and expand your field of awareness to include the entire range of experience— breath, sounds, thoughts, images, sensations, and emotions.

Fully experience anything that arises into your consciousness, letting your mind settle without wavering, wherever it goes.

Ending Your Practice

Ending your meditation session is as important as the meditation itself. A thoughtless transition from meditation to ordinary consciousness may generate discomforts like irritability, stress or headaches. Therefore it is important to take care when you end your meditation— coming out too quickly can ruin a perfectly good meditation. When its time to end your meditation, be aware that you're going to end your meditation soon. Your body will immediately shift gears from a meditative mood to neutral gear.

Don't hurry out of your practice. Take a minute to transition gradually after meditation before opening your eyes or standing up.

Shift your focus from inward to outward. Be conscious of your surrounding.

Open your eyes a little, then close. Open your eyes again— a little more. Stay seated for half a minute. Now move your upper body slowly and gently— head, neck, shoulders... do a seated spinal twist of some kind. Stretch your arms.

Move your lower body— start with your toes. Then gently move your feet, ankles, and legs. Now stand up.

A good closing ritual helps you to absorb the full benefit of your practice.

Chapter 6: History Of Meditation

The word 'meditation' is derived from the Latin words 'meditari' (which may be translated as 'to think'; 'to dwell upon'; or 'to exercise the mind').

The origin of meditation stems from ancient beliefs that make up the component of Eastern religions. Its practice has been going on for over 5,000 years. Some of the popular religions known to practice meditation are Buddhism and Hinduism. These two religions are considered to be the oldest religions that focus on meditation as a spiritual practice. There are several forms of meditation that are practiced by the different sects of Hinduism. Principal of them is the Yoga, one of the six schools of Hindu philosophy. It provides several types of meditation that Hindu believers and even a number of Western adherents have learnt to practice.

Some of the well-known Hindu texts include the Vedas and the Yoga Sutras which was written by Patanjali. But no one has arguably been more influential in the world of meditation than Siddharta Gautama, otherwise known as Buddha. In 500 BC, he achieved enlightenment through the practice of meditation. His influence spread throughout Asia and eventually to the whole world.

While the East has been practicing meditation for several centuries already, the Western world picked the practice up much later. In fact, it was only in the mid-20th century that meditation became a popular practice among Westerners.

Today, numerous meditation centers and countless organizations have cropped up in the West. While ancient meditation practices used to be intertwined with religious practices, a good number of Western meditation centers are stripped of this spiritual aspect. In today's rapidly changing fast paced world, they now usually focus exclusively on the health benefits of this practice.

But regardless of the loss of the spiritual side of meditation, it is still widely-recognized for its benefits of mental well-being. It was and still remains to be one of the central aspects of meditation.

In Hinduism, the object of meditation is to achieve a calm state of mind. In the Yoga Sutras, there are five different states of mind being described. There is the Ksipta which describes an agitated state of mind that is unable to think, listen or remain quiet. Then there is the Mudha, a state of mind where no information seems to reach into the brain. The

Viksipta is considered as a higher state of mind where information may reach the mind but it is not able to process it. In this state, the mind moves from one thought to another and in a confused inner speech. In Ekagra the mind is pointed on a single goal. It concentrates only in one direction where as in Nirodhah the mind is under complete control.

When it comes to meditation, different beliefs hold different spiritual and psychological practices in order to develop or achieve a higher degree of mental consciousness and awareness. Many religions have developed their own method and technique of meditation that allows their adherents to arrive at a higher state of consciousness.

The differences of the techniques used may be classified according to their focus. There are certain techniques that focus on a certain perception or experience while there are others that focus on a specific object to achieve a higher consciousness. There are also some forms of meditation that combine the use of open focus and the use of a specific object for focus in their practice to achieve a higher state of consciousness.

In western world mindfulness is the style of meditation that has spread like a wild fire. This started in the 20th century and is extremely popular as a daily routine for many people today. To put in simple words, meditation is both an ancient spiritual practice and a contemporary mind-body technique for relaxing the body and calming the mind. Instead of looking at meditation more as a spiritual experience, secular meditation emphasizes on relaxation, stress reduction and self-improvement. Meditation is as universal as art and there are many manifestations of this form of creativity. Some are superficial and others plunge the depths. There is a sense of natural ease and an innate stillness, which exists in both.

There are many types of meditation. Several meditation techniques help you to calm the mind and remain peaceful. Whereas meditation practices like Transcendental meditation helps you to transcend and reach the higher state of consciousness. There are meditation techniques that help you to lead the life you wish to lead by implanting your sub conscious with your wants and desires. This is done methodically through guided meditation practices. All these forms of meditation have been discussed in detail in the forthcoming chapters.

When meditation reached the western shores eminent psychologists and doctors decided to simplify it, yet maintain the essence to make it attractive for the western audience. That is how Mindfulness came into practice. Using scientific methods the psychologists made an amalgamation of various meditation practices and simply called it Mindfulness. In this practice the person performing meditation is fully aware of what is going on in his mind. Continuous practice of Mindfulness will help you gain mind control and steer your thoughts in the direction you wish them to go. Jon Kabat Zinn at University of Massachusetts Medical center developed this cognitive therapy which uses a combination of mindfulness meditation, body awareness, and yoga to help people become more mindful. The breathing techniques help to relieve stress and tension and relax the person to lead a stress free life. Mindfulness gives importance to the inhalation and exhalation process where in you are mindful of your senses and your breathing, your body and thoughts.

Vipassana, a Buddhist form of meditation is similar to mindfulness and so is Sudharshan Kriya, practiced by Art of Living Foundation founded by Sri Sri Ravishankar.

This amazing practice has helped many mental health patients, prisoners as well as common people to get rid of their illness and negative thoughts to lead a relaxed and satisfied life. Let us now take a look at how you can move from a mindlessness state to mindfulness state.

Chapter 7: Common Mindfulness Myths

The concept of 'Mindfulness' is making news everywhere, even appearing in Time magazine in recent history. At the center of this practice lies simply paying attention to what is happening right now, in the present. This means anything from a bodily sensation, to a scent, a taste, sound, or something you are looking at. This could also mean your thoughts and emotions. The entry of mindfulness into the mainstream spotlight is undoubtedly a good thing, as scientific research has even supported its benefits to health. However, there are some common mindfulness myths that should be cleared up before you proceed any further in this journey.

The First Mindfulness Myth: It has Nothing to do with Ethics.

Buddha was not just a teacher of the concept of being mindful, he was specific that people should follow mindfulness in a skillful, wholesome, and right way. The practice of being mindful is entirely connected with whoever is practicing this way of life, and their personal intentions and thoughts.

Causing no Harm: This concept is related to the idea of causing no harm, or as little as possible. Someone who uses extreme focus to harm others is not following "right" mindfulness, which is caring about other living beings. This also means taking care of yourself as well as extending kindness to others. Focusing with Care: Mindfulness can be defined as giving caring focus to the now. Caring focus means having intentions that don't cause harm to others, and choosing kindness, generosity, and compassion toward all living things, including yourself.

This means that when you witness someone suffering, while you're in a state of mindfulness, you should do whatever you are able to do to aid that person, whether it's a small gesture or not.

Knowing when to Take Action: This way of approaching mindfulness does not just sit idly by and watch when something bad happens. You must use your brain to know when you should move from passive observation to action. Many actions can be positive, such as rescuing a person from harm's way.

Recognizing Unhealthy Behaviors: Finally, when you give your environment caring focus, you can better notice which of your habits or actions are causing you harm. For example, you might have an addiction to unhealthy foods, but it is not caring focus to obsess over the junk food aisle at your grocery store.

The Second Mindfulness Myth: This Concept Clashes with Some Religions.

Mindfulness does not belong to a certain system of belief, or just one religion, even if it was popularized originally by Buddha. Mindfulness is a method for improving your mind and life by figuring out how to engage with your present moments as they pass by. There is no reason why this technique should only be reserved for certain people. Everyone can benefit from the practice of being mindful.

The Third Mindfulness Myth: It's very Easy to be Mindful.

It sounds easy to be mindful of your surroundings and mind, but the truth is, that's not always the case. At times, it can be easy, but others, it's harder.

Remembering the Practice: Since most of us are in a habit of being constantly distracted by the ruckus our mind and thoughts, the hardest part of mindfulness is simply remembering to do it. The good news is, it gets easier and easier the more you do it, like any other habit.

Building up a Mind Muscle: At first, the practice of mindfulness seems fresh and, at times, exciting, but it's important to stick with it even after that initial excitement starts to wear off. Consider it as building up a mind muscle. The stronger it gets, the easier it will be to stick with it through the tougher times.

The Fourth Mindfulness Myth: This Practice only goes with Meditation.

Some believe that mindfulness should only be practiced along with meditation, but that simply isn't the case. Actually, at retreats mindfulness is just as important outside of the practice of meditation as inside of it. At these retreats, the members are asked to do all activities with mindfulness, including eating, chores, and walking. Doing will ensure that you:

Are More Aware of your Activities: Making sure you practice mindfulness, not only during meditation, but throughout all of your daily activities, will help you remain aware.

Figure out the Way your Mind Functions: When you commit to staying mindful throughout all of your activities, you will notice how often the chattering of your mind distracts you from enjoying your experiences.

Have a Quieter and More Focused Mind: As soon as you stay aware of the chatter going on in your mind as it comes up, you will notice that you experience quiet periods more and more often. This will allow you to take a break from this intrusive pattern and enjoy your surroundings.

This being said, you should definitely remember that the practice of mindfulness is not meant to free you completely from your mind or thoughts, since that is not possible. Instead, you should try to notice what is happening inside of you, whether it's a thought, an itch, or a smell. Getting into this habit will ensure that you can use your mind when you wish to use it, instead of feeling trapped by it and unable to escape.

The Fifth Mindfulness Myth: Mindfulness is the Same as Joyfulness.

Some think that being mindful is simply a quick route to instant joy, and although it does help you feel happier with life, in general, it isn't always sunshine and roses. Noticing the now when you are in physical pain or have just argued with a loved one is not the same as experiencing joy. To put it another way, the now is not constantly pleasant. But mindfulness can be the same as learning to view your current circumstances with acceptance and peace.

Ignorance does not Mean Bliss: Ignoring a situation when something goes wrong only intensifies the dissatisfaction that you will experience at that time. On the other hand, learning to stay in the now as you experience different mental states and staying in a non-judgmental head space can ensure peace.

Pain is a Part of Life: On certain days, the now might come with heartache or a headache. Staying in the now and being mindful helps this by allowing you to assess your life with compassion and an open mind, even if this includes emotional or physical pain. Pain is simply a part of life, and mindfulness will help you realize that.

In this practice, experiences that are negative or positive are seen as the same and treated with kindness and a friendly open heart. This is the beauty of learning to be present; you no longer condemn certain experiences while welcoming others, it's all just what is happening in your life at that time.

The Sixth Mindfulness Myth: This Practice is Passive.

Some people believe that simply observing yourself and your environment is a passive way to live. Although the practice of mindfulness can be seen as something passive, in order to calm yourself and relax (which is beneficial to your health), it is also a way to gain insight and wisdom. You have access to information that allows you to learn all about yourself and reality. Here are some ways that mindfulness is anything but passive:

Investigation into Yourself: Mindfulness is all about investigation and curiosity, which leads to peace with the now. This investigation is anything but passive, since you have to stay alert, aware, and cognizant of what is happening at all times. This isn't always so easy to do, as any person dedicated to mindfulness can tell you. However, it's well worth the benefits you gain from it.

Noticing your Patterns of Clinging: When you watch your mind in a present way, you notice the way your conditioned patterns work. Most of us have a tendency to cling onto and grasp nice experiences or memories, while wishing to avoid or resist experiences that we see as negative. The fact is, however, that negative states are just a part of living. Resistance causes more harm than good. Letting Go: When you use the power of the present moment and stay mindful, you will be able to notice why you usually feel dissatisfied, anxious, or uneasy throughout your daily life. As you practice more and more, you will start to be aware by default, and then you can finally decide to let go the mental patterns that do not serve you. All of that resistance and clinging is exhausting, and when you learn to finally let go of this, you will experience great relief and an opening of your heart, which brings well-being and peace.

Mindfulness is a valuable tool and practice, during meditation and outside of it, that allows you to see how your emotions and thoughts function on a day to day basis. When you start to notice the way you grasp nice experiences and avoid or resist negative ones, you will see how this makes you needlessly unhappy and stressed out. Eventually, you will be able to reside in a more peaceful frame of mind. This is constant work and practice, but you will find that it pays off.

Chapter 8: Understanding Your Current Situation

The first step in practicing mindfulness is evaluating your life and understanding where all the stress is coming from. This, after all, was how Buddha began his teachings -- by making people understand why they suffer. And since mindfulness is rooted in Buddhism, this book will follow the same course to help you, at the very least, achieve peace.

The sufferings mentioned in the Four Noble Truths of Buddhism are pain, illness, aging and death. Every fear swimming in every person's head is rooted in these four. Since, however, the main goal of this book is to simply lift you from everyday stress and not lead you to enlightenment, it's enough that you settle with the details

-- which environments snap your stress, which people raise your temper, what situations trigger anxieties, and such.

Understand that people live different lives. Simply because work is the source of stress of one, it does not mean it's yours too. It could be your family, your relationship, the landlord, the reflection on the mirror, and several other factors.

Why is this important?

Mindfulness is attained through meditation. Although it seems simple and effortless (all you need to do is sit down and do nothing after all), it's actually not. There are lots going on inside -- physically, mentally and emotionally -- and these can make a short five minute session extremely arduous, especially for beginners.

A considerable number of people have failed in this basic exercise. Most claimed it's difficult and ineffective, but in reality, they simply failed to select the right environment, schedule, or one of the several other factors needed to consider before indulging in meditation. As a result, instead of inching slowly towards peace, they fall over and over on frustration.

Meditation shall be further discussed in Chapter 3.

Your First Mindfulness Exercise

Essentially, this is more of a reflection. You will observe yourself throughout the day, and take note of what emotions (negative and positive) have risen during significant events. Know that mindfulness is not yet applied in this exercise because that will require a certain degree of control over your emotions. Whereas in reflections, you are free to think and feel whatever you want.

You will need a notebook, smartphone, or anything that can keep notes close by. As you go about your day, list reflections and observations down as you would in a diary. Keep everything brief, however. If possible, limit your sentences to two; the first, describing the event, place or person, then on the second, how you felt about it. If you are the type of person who can manage to keep all notes in memory, then you may skip the notebook. As long as you can recall your highs and lows later on, that's good enough.

The following questions are but mere guides, and should not necessarily be answered. These are merely aimed to help you determine which events of the day should be observed and given significance.

- How do you feel in the morning? Do you feel eager to start the day? Or would rather stay in bed?

- What pushes you to get out of bed and start the day? Your energized kids or dog, breakfast, work, your significant other, etc.?

- Are you fond of your home? Or do you always find your feet itching to leave?

- How do you feel during travels from home to work and vice versa? Do you feel stressed or panicked as you make your way through busy streets? Do you feel enraged by the drive home and the traffic that comes along?

- How do you feel or act upon arriving at work? Do you dive immediately in your tasks? Or do you linger with officemates for a while, proceeding only to your cubicle once the boss arrives?

- Do you love your job? Are you in it because of the money, the super cool boss, or the love for what you're doing?

- How do you spend your free time, and how do you feel about the activity?

- How is your relationship with friends, family, co-workers, and significant other? Is there anyone you don't look forward seeing throughout the day? The landlord, that nosy client, the ex, the creepy taco seller across the street, etc.?

- Who or what are the things that push you to do the things you do?

- What part of the day do you look forward to? Dinner, sleeping, shower, exercise, the walk with your dog, playtime with your kids, etc.?

- What is your favorite place, and how do you feel whenever you spend time there?

Tip! Keep this practice for at least a week. Moods and emotions vary day to day, so you need to ascertain how you truly feel towards a situation, event, person, or place. For example, the simple reason why you could be feeling really good one morning is because of an unexpected pat on the back from a respected superior the day before.

There are dozens more possible questions that can help you reflect. Therefore, if you think there are more about you or your life that aren't asked but are worth noting down, feel free to do so.

Chapter 9: Benefits

The Benefits of Being Mindful

Being mindful in your life has many benefits both the short-term and long-term. When you are psychologically aware of every moment you experience in life, it becomes rather enriching.

Complete awareness every day is not a waste. It can transform you, change your outlook, improve your general well-being and assure you a brighter future. When you are living in the present instead of passing your day nonchalantly, your life can be simpler.

Before I go into the short-term and long-term benefit of mindfulness, I want you to understand what happens when you are not practicing mindful living. When you know the opposite, you can appreciate the benefits.

If you live without paying attention or being aware, the following occur:

1. You lose the connection with your true person.

2. The energy to continue will not be present.

3. The choice making process will cease to matter.

4. Performance effectiveness is drastically reduced.

5. Your reaction to situations will be full of criticism and judgments.

6. Compassion and gratitude disappears from your character.

7. Living to the fullest becomes impossible.

Absentminded living can be terrible, but when you are always aware of what your life is and the direction you are moving in, you will gain, not lose. Let's see what happens with mindful living.

Short-Term Benefits

1. You can be your true self

Mindful living allows you to live in the present and savor every moment of your life. When you are fully aware of everything you are doing, you will not act according to the thoughts, roles, and feelings that don't relate to your present existence. Instead, you can easily understand your values and also respond positively to what your true self needs.

2. You will have more control over your life

When you are mindful of the life you are living, controlling your actions, thinking pattern and making the right choices will be easier. Instead of acting on what others, situation and society demands, you can do those things that will develop you and help you live a happier life.

3.Your performance will improve

Distraction affects the output you deliver every day. When you are living mindfully, you will be completely aware, focused, energized, resourceful and free from pressure. Since you can control your physiological and psychological state, it will be easy to change them whenever they are debilitating or unproductive.

4.Your ability to understand will increase

If you are present, you will have the relevant information from your inner mind and your experience. You will also be ready to listen to others and evaluate your immediate environment. It will be easy to understand things.

5.Your vitality, physical health, and beauty will improve

In the state of mindfulness, you are aware of your body and what it needs. You can easily interpret each signal and satisfy it. In a state of mindfulness, every bite you take adds value as you are aware of what you are eating and will ensure, you are eating healthy. f you continue to do that every day, everything about you will change. You will notice a significant change in your health. There will be a spring in your step.

6.Inner strength, peace, and happiness

Living a mindful life can help you push out those emotions, impulses, and thoughts that make you anxious all the time and in a negative frame of mind. As you free your mind from that garbage, you can be at peace within which will lead to strength and happiness.

7.Your relationships with others will be healthier and more successful

I don't know about you, but people don't like to be treated casually and ignored. It doesn't matter whether they are family, colleagues or friends. Everyone wants someone who can identify and appreciate their true value. When you listen, relate, empathize and appreciate others, it keeps the relationship healthy.

The only way to achieve this is by being present whenever you are with others through mindful living.

8.You can be grateful and appreciative of little things

If you are living a fully-aware life, you will always find the time to thank someone for that little assistance they offered to you. You may not have observed, but when you appreciate others, they tend to do more than you ask.

Also, mindful living will help you to appreciate the good things of life like the air you breathe, the family you have, the friends that come around and even your boss that encourages you.

Long-Term Benefits

Apart from the short-term benefits of mindful living, there are many things that you stand to gain in the long-run because of this lifestyle.

1.Reduced Stress

This should be the number one long-term benefit of a mindful life. When you consider some of the things that cause stress like worries and regrets, you can understand that if you focus your life on the moment you have, the stress in your body will reduce.

A study which was conducted by Donald, Atkins, Christie & Ryan in 2016 proved that present-moment awareness facilitates responses that will help you to adapt to the daily stressors around you. Also, a study conducted by Atkins and Donald in 2016 showed that mindful living helps people to develop the ability to cope more with stress than avoid it entirely. In fact, the study found evidence that mindfulness is more effective than self-affirmation controls and relaxation when you want to fight stress.

When you live a fully-aware lifestyle, it will help you to alleviate stress by improving the regulation of your emotions which will enhance your mood and help you to handle stress.

2.Mindful living enhances your illness handling abilities

A group of people for whom mindfulness in handling illness is essential is those battling with cancer and other chronic or terminal diseases. It is true that being mindful will not remove the symptoms, but it will help them to manage it effectively.

Some studies on the effects of mindfulness on cancer patients proved that it helped them to reduce stress, enhanced their spirituality, quickened post-traumatic growth, relived fatigue and enhanced their vigor. (Zernicke, Campbell, Speca, ruff, Tamagawa, & Carlson, 2016).

3. Mindfulness facilitates recovery

Some chronic illnesses can be healed through mindful living. It doesn't stop at helping you to manage it but can also lead to full recovery.

A study which was conducted on young women who survived breast cancer proved that practicing mindful living can increase self-kindness, decrease stress and decrease rumination. (Boyle, Stanton, Ganz, Crespi, & Bower, 2017).

4. Mindfulness reduces the symptoms of depression

Living a mindful life can treat depression which can lead to suicide and death. According to Falsafi, 2016, a mindful lifestyle can increase self-compassion and reduce depressive symptoms.

A mindful life enables the practitioner to regulate his/her emotions. It also enhances their ability to identify and regulate extreme negative emotions instead of allowing themselves to fall victim to it.

5. It improves general lifestyle and health

Living a life that is aware of every moment can help someone to live healthy, safe and sound. When you are in the present, it will become easy to identify the need for regular check-ups, the importance of driving with seat belts, dangers of alcohol and nicotine, and the benefits of physical activities. (Jacobs, Wollny, Sim & Horsch, 2016).

Short-term and Long-term benefits of mindfulness can change an ordinary busy and dull life to an interesting and vigorous life filled with happiness and satisfaction. On a general note, mindful living can also help people:

a. To improve their mental health

b. Reduce anxiety

c. Eliminate race and age bias

d. Improve cognition

e. Enhance satisfaction

f. Reduce distractions

The practice is simple, but the benefits are numerous. You too can start living a life that is mindful instead of allowing the issues of life to weigh you down. No matter how busy you are, make time for who you are and change your life for good.

Chapter 10: Yoga Meditation

Yoga is currently very popular. Following are a few descriptions of how you can blend the practice of mindfulness meditation with yoga asanas.

Savasana: Savasana is also called the corpse pose. When practicing you have to lie on your back, keep your arms at your side a few inches away from your upper body with palms facing up and keeping your feet 12 to 18 inches apart. Completely surrender your body to the existing gravitational pull. Focus on your breathing, be aware of your inbreath and the outbreath. Notice the overall state of your body as well. Is your body is completely relaxed or some part is still tense? When your mind wanders, (as expected) observe where it went without any judgment and bring your focus to your breathing.

Suchirandrasana: You have already practiced the corpse position. Now from that position bring both your feet to the ground close to your buttocks, keep your hip width apart. Draw your left knee toward your chest and place your outer right shin to your left thigh. With your right arm, reach between your legs and with your left arm, reach the outside of your left leg and clasp your arms. Allow your breath to flow naturally, and don't try to change it. You might feel some stretching sensations in your right hip depending on the openness of your body. The surrounding muscles might tense as well. Maintain the stretch that you have engineered and release the tension and watch how the sensations change. Practice the very same thing on the other side of your body. You might find that your one hip generates more sensations than others. As always, when any distracting thoughts and feelings arise, simply observe and don't judge or analyze them.

Bitilasana: Stand on the floor, and get onto your hands and knees. Position your knees under your hips and your hands directly under your shoulders. When you breathe out, round the back and scoop the tail bone between your legs. Tilt your head so that you can gaze back between your thighs. When you breathe in, create a subtle backbend by positioning your belly to the floor, tilting your pelvis forward and letting your spine move into your torso. Make sure you position your tail bone and the crown of your head towards the ceiling. Avoid reaching upwards with your chin because it will compress the back of your neck. Focus on your breath and coordinate your movements with the breathing while you rock back and forth a few times. After a few minutes, you will find that your mind starts to wander. Observe where it went and return your attention to the practice.

Chapter 11: How Does Mindfulness Help You?

Being happy in any given moment – being present in this moment – that is all we need to lead a healthy, cheerful and peaceful life. Science actually suggests that the benefits of mindfulness can be phenomenal. Increasing our capacity for mindfulness supports many attitudes that contribute to a satisfied life.

Being mindful makes it easier to savor the pleasures in life as they occur, helps us become fully engaged in activities and creates a greater capacity to deal with adverse events. By focusing on the now, we will find ourselves getting lesser caught in the worries. We will remain less preoccupied; we will be able to establish a deeper connection with ourselves and others.

And when we are mindful to this extent, life becomes utmost joyous and fulfilling.

Mindfulness for physical health

Mindfulness can improve our physical health in various ways. Being mindful helps to:

Eat right

Prevent obesity

Shed excess pounds

Curtail the risk of cardiovascular diseases

Regulate levels of stress

Manage blood pressure levels

Reduce chronic pain and inflammatory conditions such as fibromyalgia

Improve sleep

Offer relief from gastrointestinal disorders

Enhance sexual life

Offer relief from post-traumatic stress disorder induced physical ailments

Slow down neurodegenerative diseases

Mindfulness for mental health

According to psychotherapists who are using mindfulness meditation as a powerful healing tool, being mindfulness could bring in positive changes in a myriad of mental issues. Some of the areas that benefit from this include:

Depression

Eating disorders

Anxiety and panic attacks

Obsessive compulsive disorder

Post-traumatic stress disorders

Alcohol/drug abuse

Childhood abuse

Sexual abuse

In the aforementioned cases, being mindful has proven to be helpful to inculcate:

Positive mood changes

Lesser mood swings

Improved relationships

Better self-compassion

Better levels of empathy and sympathy

Lesser levels of anxiety

Lesser anger and frustrations

Better relaxation

Being mindful also helps to improve:

Concentration

Focus

Memory

Learning skills

Attention

Emotional intelligence

Creativity

Resilience

Decision making skills

Analytical skills

Mindfulness for spirituality

Mindfulness and spirituality share a very close-knit relationship. The former is the ultimate tool to master self-cultivated spirituality. So how does mindfulness help our spiritual life and cherish our soul? It helps us to:

Stay grounded

Stay unperturbed irrespective of the situation we are in

Understand and act in a calm, serene way during turbulent times

Practice forgiveness

Let go of the past

Release anything and everything that does not serve us

Bond closely with our True or Higher Self

Remain unattached, yet remain happy

Be self-compassionate

Love ourselves unconditionally

Face fear and let go of it without coming under its clutches

According to studies, people who practice mindfulness regularly age more slowly than the non-practitioners. In simple words, it improves our overall quality of life across all realms of our lives as we are living and savoring this moment without judging and criticizing, and just by accepting the moment without attaching any strings.

When we become mindful, we will become exponentially more effective in life and discover the difference between fleeting happiness and continual-enduring joy. So just let go of the 'was' and surrender to the 'is'...

Chapter 12: Understanding Past And Future

Most people spend their time thinking about the past or worrying about the future. The past feels very real to most people, where is the past? Let's really take a look at this concept. A common answer that comes up is: the past is behind me. Look behind you right now. Where is the past? It's gone. Gone where? In the past. But where??? No where. It doesn't exist. If I offered to pay you 10 million dollars to go back to 1:00 pm yesterday, you couldn't do it. No matter how hard you tried, you'd realize that there is no where to get to because it doesn't exist. Once the moment passes, it's gone. We hold on to the concept of the past like it's a real place to get to, but it's nothing more than a concept.

The only time that ever exists is the 'now'. Our minds make the past feel like it's very real. A key point to making mindfulness work is fully accepting that the past is completely insubstantial because it is not real, it does not exist. Some people misinterpret this to mean denial of the past. This is not denial. This is just realizing what is is, and what isn't isn't. The now 'is' and the past 'isn't'. So when the past comes up, ask yourself if you really need to be thinking about that right now. More often than not, the answer is no.

The future has no existence except as a thought. Your mind believes it is something else, something real to get to and that once you get there, you'll be happy, or you'll finally love yourself or be okay with yourself. The hope is that at some point in the future, the problem of your 'self' will be resolved.

Losing control of your memory (past) and your imagination (future, anxiety).

The past does not exist unless you create a thought about the past. There is no past. And you can only think that thought about the past now. You can never access the past or the future, because they don't exist. Where are they? They are only thoughts. Time is a man made concept that only exists as a thought.

The link between past and future and mental health

Depression and anxiety are the most common mental illnesses in the world. When you think about distressing events that happened in the past, that's depression. In psychology we call it morbid rumination. You just relive the past experience over and over in your mind, wishing it had been different. This type of thinking has no impact on the actual events. It renders you powerless because you're spending mental energy trying to impact something that no longer exists. You can't change the past, but you can impact the now. Accept what happened, and ask 'what now?'. Acceptance does not mean you approve or even think it's okay, it just means acknowledging that what happened happened. It's saying yes to what happened. Saying no to what happened is torturous because we know it happened, but we're stuck wishing it hadn't happened. That is a sure way to suffer forever. Say yes to what happened. Take the judgment out of it (liking or disliking what happened). You can't move forward without acceptance.

The next question is, where is the future? The future feels very real to most people as well. But where is it? Again, only in our imaginations. We can only imagine the future, but we can't ever live in the future. Any distressing, worrying thought about the future is anxiety. Anxiety is worrying about what is not happening.

Although the concept of the future seems very real, the future only ever happens in the now. Try to get to 5 minutes from now. Even if someone offered you 10 million dollars to get to the future (5 minutes from now) you wouldn't be able to do it. When 5 minutes comes, you will experience it in the now. Never as the future. There is no real future. There's just the present moment. Just the now.

depression peace anxiety

past presentfuture

To recap, depression always involves past-based thinking. Ruminating about distressing thoughts about the past, thinking why did they do this, or why did I do that. Wishing it was different. Anxiety always involves future-based thinking.

Anxiety can vary from worrying about what will happen in a specific situation like planning a date and worrying that it will go wrong, saying something stupid at a business meeting, to more general thoughts like "my life is over", "I've ruined my life", "I will never be happy", "I'm a failure".

Past-based thinking involves your memory and future-based thinking involves your imagination. They are thoughts not focused on what is actually happening in the present moment reality. Reality only exists in the present moment. Thinking about past or future is unnecessary and often delusional.

depression peace anxiety

past present future

non-reality reality non-reality

Make a commitment to only deal in reality. When distressing thoughts occur, do present moment reality checks to determine if you are dealing in reality or non-reality. Present moment reality checks include noticing where you actually are, what you are actually experiencing. For example: I'm sitting on a chair in my living room, the sun is shining through the window. The temperature is comfortable, I am safe.

Anxiety

Anxiety is a fear response in which we perceive a lack of physical or emotional safety. We experience the urge to fight, flee, or freeze. Every time we give in to the fear, it becomes stronger. We become afraid of being afraid, anxious about being anxious. The answer is: do not give in to the fear. When you give in to the fear (ex: you decide not to go to a party you really wanted to go to) you experience relief from the anxiety. However, because you experienced relief, the next time you are invited to a party it will be even harder to make yourself go because you reinforced the response that gave you relief (but it's the opposite of what you want).

Anxiety is fear of the future. You can't overcome what does not exist. Since anxiety is fear about the future, you can never overcome it because it doesn't exist. The fear exists in your imagination, but it's not actually in the world. How do you fight something that doesn't exist? Most of the things you've feared in the past never even happened. If thoughts are about the future, you can't do anything about it because it's not happening. That's why anxiety is so distressing: because you have no power to do something about something that isn't happening (non-reality).

You can only actually do something about things that are actually happening right now (reality). If there is something you can do, then take action now, and know that you've done all you can for now. Drop any other thoughts about it, recognizing that any worrying won't actually help you.

For example, you are worried that you can't pay a bill and you're going to have your electricity cut off at the end of the month. You worry, worry, worry. Ask yourself: is there anything I can do about it right now? You may be able to call the company and ask for an extension, you may be able to call a friend and ask if you can borrow the money, you may be able to pick up a side job to make some extra money. Those are actions you can take right now. Once you've done all you can, drop it. Notice that right now, you still have electricity. If it gets to the point where the worst case scenario has happened, the lights are cut off, then you will handle it at that time. Right now, the lights are on.

Life grants you the grace of one moment at a time. You don't have to worry about the rest of your life because life unfolds only in this moment. Can you handle this moment? Yes? Then you can handle your life. One moment at a time.

Planning

Does staying in the present moment mean that you can't plan for the future? Not at all! For practical purposes, planning and setting goals is beneficial.

How to plan: Just say you want to go to New York next month. You will need to make travel arrangements. You look at the calendar and select the dates. This part of the process requires planning into the future, which is completely appropriate. In the now, you may purchase your airline tickets and book your hotel. Then that's it. No more thinking is required. What often happens is you start worrying about it. What if I miss my flight, what if something goes wrong? That is the unnecessary thinking about the future that most people engage in. That's when you bring yourself back to the present moment and tell yourself, "I don't need to think about that right now, because it isn't happening."

Another example could be you decide to go back to school. Planning for the future is appropriate as you submit your application and select the courses you'll take. Then that's it. No more future is required. Just attend the classes when it's time to attend the classes. No worries about 'what if I don't pass, what if I'm not smart enough, what if I fail?' Bring yourself back to the present moment. Ask yourself if you need to be thinking about that right now.

Chapter 13: Understanding Past And

Future

Most people spend their time thinking about the past or worrying about the future. The past feels very real to most people, where is the past? Let's really take a look at this concept. A common answer that comes up is: the past is behind me. Look behind you right now. Where is the past? It's gone. Gone where? In the past. But where??? No where. It doesn't exist. If I offered to pay you 10 million dollars to go back to 1:00 pm yesterday, you couldn't do it. No matter how hard you tried, you'd realize that there is no where to get to because it doesn't exist. Once the moment passes, it's gone. We hold on to the concept of the past like it's a real place to get to, but it's nothing more than a concept.

The only time that ever exists is the 'now'. Our minds make the past feel like it's very real. A key point to making mindfulness work is fully accepting that the past is completely insubstantial because it is not real, it does not exist. Some people misinterpret this to mean denial of the past. This is not denial. This is just realizing what is is, and what isn't isn't. The now 'is' and the past 'isn't'. So when the past comes up, ask yourself if you really need to be thinking about that right now. More often than not, the answer is no.

The future has no existence except as a thought. Your mind believes it is something else, something real to get to and that once you get there, you'll be happy, or you'll finally love yourself or be okay with yourself. The hope is that at some point in the future, the problem of your 'self' will be resolved.

Losing control of your memory (past) and your imagination (future, anxiety).

The past does not exist unless you create a thought about the past. There is no past. And you can only think that thought about the past now. You can never access the past or the future, because they don't exist. Where are they? They are only thoughts. Time is a man made concept that only exists as a thought.

The link between past and future and mental health

Depression and anxiety are the most common mental illnesses in the world. When you think about distressing events that happened in the past, that's depression. In psychology we call it morbid rumination. You just relive the past experience over and over in your mind, wishing it had been different. This type of thinking has no impact on the actual events. It renders you powerless because you're spending mental energy trying to impact something that no longer exists. You can't change the past, but you can impact the now. Accept what happened, and ask 'what now?'. Acceptance does not mean you approve or even think it's okay, it just means acknowledging that what happened happened. It's saying yes to what happened. Saying no to what happened is torturous because we know it happened, but we're stuck wishing it hadn't happened. That is a sure way to suffer forever. Say yes to what happened. Take the judgment out of it (liking or disliking what happened). You can't move forward without acceptance.

The next question is, where is the future? The future feels very real to most people as well. But where is it? Again, only in our imaginations. We can only imagine the future, but we can't ever live in the future. Any distressing, worrying thought about the future is anxiety. Anxiety is worrying about what is not happening.

Although the concept of the future seems very real, the future only ever happens in the now. Try to get to 5 minutes from now. Even if someone offered you 10 million dollars to get to the future (5 minutes from now) you wouldn't be able to do it. When 5 minutes comes, you will experience it in the now. Never as the future. There is no real future. There's just the present moment. Just the now.

depression peace anxiety

past presentfuture

To recap, depression always involves past-based thinking. Ruminating about distressing thoughts about the past, thinking why did they do this, or why did I do that. Wishing it was different. Anxiety always involves future-based thinking.

Anxiety can vary from worrying about what will happen in a specific situation like planning a date and worrying that it will go wrong, saying something stupid at a business meeting, to more general thoughts like "my life is over", "I've ruined my life", "I will never be happy", "I'm a failure".

Past-based thinking involves your memory and future-based thinking involves your imagination. They are thoughts not focused on what is actually happening in the present moment reality. Reality only exists in the present moment. Thinking about past or future is unnecessary and often delusional.

depression peace anxiety

past present future

non-reality reality non-reality

Make a commitment to only deal in reality. When distressing thoughts occur, do present moment reality checks to determine if you are dealing in reality or non-reality. Present moment reality checks include noticing where you actually are, what you are actually experiencing. For example: I'm sitting on a chair in my living room, the sun is shining through the window. The temperature is comfortable, I am safe.

Anxiety

Anxiety is a fear response in which we perceive a lack of physical or emotional safety. We experience the urge to fight, flee, or freeze. Every time we give in to the fear, it becomes stronger. We become afraid of being afraid, anxious about being anxious. The answer is: do not give in to the fear. When you give in to the fear (ex: you decide not to go to a party you really wanted to go to) you experience relief from the anxiety. However, because you experienced relief, the next time you are invited to a party it will be even harder to make yourself go because you reinforced the response that gave you relief (but it's the opposite of what you want).

Anxiety is fear of the future. You can't overcome what does not exist. Since anxiety is fear about the future, you can never overcome it because it doesn't exist. The fear exists in your imagination, but it's not actually in the world. How do you fight something that doesn't exist? Most of the things you've feared in the past never even happened. If thoughts are about the future, you can't do anything about it because it's not happening. That's why anxiety is so distressing: because you have no power to do something about something that isn't happening (non-reality).

You can only actually do something about things that are actually happening right now (reality). If there is something you can do, then take action now, and know that you've done all you can for now. Drop any other thoughts about it, recognizing that any worrying won't actually help you.

For example, you are worried that you can't pay a bill and you're going to have your electricity cut off at the end of the month. You worry, worry, worry. Ask yourself: is there anything I can do about it right now? You may be able to call the company and ask for an extension, you may be able to call a friend and ask if you can borrow the money, you may be able to pick up a side job to make some extra money. Those are actions you can take right now. Once you've done all you can, drop it. Notice that right now, you still have electricity. If it gets to the point where the worst case scenario has happened, the lights are cut off, then you will handle it at that time. Right now, the lights are on.

Life grants you the grace of one moment at a time. You don't have to worry about the rest of your life because life unfolds only in this moment. Can you handle this moment? Yes? Then you can handle your life. One moment at a time.

Planning

Does staying in the present moment mean that you can't plan for the future? Not at all! For practical purposes, planning and setting goals is beneficial.

How to plan: Just say you want to go to New York next month. You will need to make travel arrangements. You look at the calendar and select the dates. This part of the process requires planning into the future, which is completely appropriate. In the now, you may purchase your airline tickets and book your hotel. Then that's it. No more thinking is required. What often happens is you start worrying about it. What if I miss my flight, what if something goes wrong? That is the unnecessary thinking about the future that most people engage in. That's when you bring yourself back to the present moment and tell yourself, "I don't need to think about that right now, because it isn't happening."

Another example could be you decide to go back to school. Planning for the future is appropriate as you submit your application and select the courses you'll take. Then that's it. No more future is required. Just attend the classes when it's time to attend the classes. No worries about 'what if I don't pass, what if I'm not smart enough, what if I fail?' Bring yourself back to the present moment. Ask yourself if you need to be thinking about that right now.

Chapter 14: Mindfulness Exercises For Beginners!

Mindfulness Exercises for Beginners!

Here are mindfulness exercises to help you find the path towards a mindful life. You don't need to perform or know each of these mindfulness exercises. Try a few and go from there.

1. Mindful Awareness - Gives you a deeper appreciation and awareness of even the simplest of tasks. Start this exercise by focusing on something you do each day. Start this task and while doing it take a second to be mindful of where you are, how you feel in the moment, and how the task benefits you.

2. Mindful Breathing - This is the breath awareness exercise discussed at the end of

the last chapter. Start small and work your way up. Increase the time as you go on. I've worked my way up to 20 minutes a day. I also use it as a tool to center myself at random times during the day if I feel off track. Those sessions last for a shorter length of time.

3. Mindful Listening - Helps you open your ears to listening without passing judgment. What we hear is often influenced by a prior experience. Start this exercise by choosing an audio track you've never listened to. Close your eyes and put on headphones to block out any outside noise. Once you've started listening to the audio track, try to resist being drawn into any judgment of the audio track or the person who is singing. Allow yourself to follow the music while thinking of nothing besides it.

4. Mindful Observation - You can do this in both a sitting and standing position. Pick an object in your surrounding environment and focus on that object alone for 1 to 2 minutes. Only pay attention to the object you've picked to focus on. Inspect every part of your chosen object and relax into harmony for as long as you're able to concentrate.

5. Mindful Movement - This exercise requires an intentional movement. This can be walking, stretching, or yoga. Your intention while doing this exercise is to focus on your breath and body, noticing the sensations when you move and each of the moments when you remain still.

6. Mindful Immersion - This exercise teaches us to be content in any moment. It teaches us to avoid always wanting and working towards things. To start this exercise, pick a general task. Instead of

completing the task as fast as possible, take your time to appreciate each aspect of the task as you're doing it. Don't focus on finishing the task. Immerse yourself into every action the task requires you to take. Feel and become one with the motions needed to finish the task. Try to align yourself spiritually, mentally, and physically so you're completely in each moment, enjoying every action as you make it.

7. Body Scans - This exercise moves your focus to paying attention around your body, being curious during your experiences, and observing each sensation as you realize it. These meditations come in various forms and can be found online for free. They will range from a few minutes to 1 hour.

8. Sitting Meditations -This exercise can range from a few minutes to 1 hour. There

are many variations available for you to practice with. This exercise involves using your breath while in a seated position. It teaches you to become more aware of sounds, bodily sensations, thoughts, and feelings.

9. Mindful Appreciation - This exercise asks that you write down 3 to 10 things you overlook or fail to appreciate in your daily life. It doesn't matter what things you write. They can be objects or people. Once your list is completed, give thanks and appreciation to each object or person you've added to your list. The object of this exercise is to notice things that are often overlooked and taken for granted. You want to learn about these people or things and appreciate all the ways they enrich your life.

10. Guided Imagery - This exercise focuses and directs your imagination in a positive

way to help relax your body and mind. Guided imagery can be complex or simple. Guided imagery uses music and words to evoke scenarios of positive imagery. It's often referred to as visualization, although that technique is different as it involves all your emotions and senses. This exercise involves only your imagination and has been proven to positively influence a person's overall well-being and mental health.

11. Guided Meditations - This exercise is a meditation that is led by others. These are plentiful online. You can find a wide variety of guided meditations online for free or for a small charge. This exercise involves another person walking you through a set of different mindfulness exercises to help you reach a deeper meditative state. Try a few until you find a guided meditation that works best for you.

Chapter 15: The Three Universal Truths

The Thee Universal Truths are different from the Noble Truths. The Noble Truths apply to living entities in our world – the humans and animals alike, the gods and demi-gods. But the Three Universal Truths are the truths of the world itself, including living and non-living states. These are impermanence, suffering and non-self.

Anitya: **Impermanence**

Anitya recognises that nothing is permanent in this world – everything changes. In fact, the only thing that is holds a state of permanence is change itself. It refers to the ever-changing dynamic of our living world. Life does not stop, not even in the slightest. Our world is developing continuously – rivers flow, mountains form, the clouds are in motion.

Everything is constantly in a state of endless change.

To understand this truth allows one to acquire a positive outlook on life and internalise his peace. If you are able to accept impermanence in your world, you are able to understand that everything that occurs will change. It is the understanding of the belief that pain will change, life itself will change and you will be able to redirect your focus to the positive energy within.

Dukkha: **Suffering**

This truth understands how impermanence leads to suffering — nothing is invulnerable to the coming of pain. Impermanence means that everything that changes will come to suffering, and everything is changing. To believe and internalise this truth allows one to build faith in the teachings of the

Great Gautama. Dukkha allows for the realisation that Buddha's path is that to peace, harmony and enlightenment.

Anatma: **Non-Self**

This truth describes that no entity in our world may possess permanence, acting simultaneously with Anitya – nothing can possess a 'self'. Buddha does not believe these entities to exist.

Anatma recognises that the body, nor mind, can act as its 'self', but merely be attributed to it. Buddhism requires the rejection of the 'self'.

The Buddhist philosophy believes that:

'Self' leads to the failure of harmony in relationships with others. To believe in ones 'self' is to apply hierarchy to the world around – to judge others in comparison to your 'self'. To remove oneself from the belief of 'self' is allowing peace through our interactions with other people. Our selfish desires are no longer present or able to manifest within us because they cannot exist in conjunction with the 'self'-less belief. This promotes the harmony in which Buddhism aims to achieve in the lives of all people.

Enlightenment cannot then be achieved without first extinguishing the belief in 'self'. It is with the ignorance to the concept of 'self' that allows us to truly act upon generosity and equality, to express our greatest harmony to others and reach spiritual enlightenment.

The Three **Divisions** of Buddhism

Buddhism is a very widely spread and popular spiritual belief. Over the course of time, 3 significant divisions of the Buddhist faith have emerged and are widely practiced all over the world today – Theraveda, Mahyana, and Vajrayana. The division originate in the origin of the Buddhist faith, India, and have spread out throughout the modern world. It's important to understand and respect the differences in the different Buddhist faiths – all offer differences which may appeal to your individual self.

Theraveda

Theraveda Buddhism is the most dedicated division to the teachings of the Buddha himself, conforming to all the original teachings. It is reliant on the last remaining transcripts of the sayings of Buddha, the Pala Canon. In Theraveda Buddhism, Buddha is considered to be a simple man, like any other. There is no conception of higher forms like we have head so far. The focus to the Theraveda Buddhist is individual enlightenment of each and every person. Nirvana can be achieved through personal dedication and spiritual liberty.

Mahyana

Mahyana alters and introduces new teachings to the Buddhist faith. Unlike Theraveda Buddhism, the Mahyana Buddhist recognises the Great Gautama as a manifestation of divine spirit, not a mere man. The Great Gotama is the essence of the Buddha.

It is believed by the Mahyana Buddhists that the Great Gotama has not been the only manifestation of the divine. The Dalai Lama is considered to be one of the greatest and most worshipped bodhisattva. The Mahyana Buddhist incorporates the teachings of the manifestations of Buddha in to their practice, and thus their Buddhist faith is ever-evolving with new teachings and understandings of life.

Vajrayana

Vajrayana Buddhism is an extension to Mahyana Buddhism. Originating from Hindu texts, which were integrated with the Buddhist philosophy, Vajrayana is considered to be a 'shortcut to enlightenment'. This form of Buddhism often contradicts the teachings and beliefs of the other divisions. It is often studied and practiced in secret – its practices are considered to undermine the great teachings of the Great Gautama and the following manifestations of his divine spirit.

Chapter 16: Living With Intention

After you have set the intention to break your autopilot mode and begin living a life filled with mindfulness practices, you need to begin focusing on mastering living with intention. Intention is a major part of mindfulness, and it happens to be one of the biggest mindfulness practices you can possibly embark on. Living with intention is less about using specific strategies, techniques, and practices to embody mindfulness, and more about honoring yourself as a person and as a human. Although there are no physical strategies to implement, the practice of living with intention is very practical and highly necessary for living a truly mindful life.

Why Is Intention Important?

There are tens, hundreds, and maybe even thousands of different mindfulness techniques and practices available to you that can be used at any time. The thing is, you can implement as many physical strategies as you desire, but if you do not have the right intentions behind them, these strategies are not really going to do anything for you.

Intention is the entire purpose behind why you do anything that you do. When it comes to mindfulness, this purpose is essential and highly necessary, and it is crucial that you become mindful of your very intentions and how they affect everything that you do.

Think about it this way: if you take a shower in the morning and you don't think much of it, it is likely just a hygienic practice to you that is necessary to fulfill before getting ready for the day ahead of you. It is a quick chance to wash your hair, soap yourself up, and wash away any dirt from your body before you get dressed. Nothing more, nothing less.

Unless you change the intention. What if, instead of just being a necessary practice, to shower meant to give yourself time to cleanse your body? Not just with soap and shampoo, but to truly cleanse it by feeling the water rushing over you. What if you set the intention that, as the water rushed over you and down the drain, you would allow it to take away any stress or worry that you have for the day ahead and wash it down the drain with it? Or what if you set the intention that the shower would awaken every fiber in your body so that you are totally awakened and ready to face the day, with all of your senses activated and ready to be involved in the day with you?

Setting your intention allows you to take otherwise average and mundane practices and turn them into something meaningful and worth paying attention to. It helps draw you out of the autopilot mode of "I have to do this," and puts you into a state of mind where you can say "I like to do this." If you do not actually like to do certain things, then mindfulness allows you the opportunity to seek new ways to do things so that you **do** like doing them and so that it does feel good to be a part of that activity each day.

Intention is a powerful tool that gives you the opportunity to change your perspective, alter how you engage with the world around you, and give new meaning to the things you do. It is a great opportunity to awaken yourself to the world once more and really begin feeling and experiencing the world around you. This is your opportunity to turn things that are otherwise mundane and boring into fun, peaceful practices that nourish you in an entirely new way.

Through the use of intentions, showers can become a time to cleanse not only your body but your soul, and awaken you to the world around you. A sip of coffee can become a time to not only get your morning caffeine rush but to awaken your taste buds and truly taste the flavors of the bean in your cup. Driving to work can become not only a time to commute to your destination but an opportunity to really **see** the world that exists between your home and your work. Everything that you do can take on an entirely new meaning and purpose when you change your intention. Just because intention is not a physical practice like yoga, meditation, or affirmations does not mean that it does not hold an equally powerful impact on how you begin living your best life possible.

How Do I Set My Intention?

Now that you have a clear understanding of how your intention impacts your ability to live your best life possible, you are probably wondering how you can go about changing your intentions. Fortunately, if you have been living on autopilot, it is likely that you have never really taken too much time to think about or assess your intentions. This means that, when you are doing things, you likely do not have any significant intention beyond "just to get it done." This means that when you start your mindfulness practice, you are essentially starting from a clean, brand new slate. You have the opportunity to choose fresh new intentions and enforce them in your day-to-day life, without actually having to erase any old intentions to set new ones in place.

Playing with a fresh new slate can be exciting and enjoyable. The number of intentions you may choose to set upon your activities is limitless, and entirely up to you. This means that you are the only one who truly gets to determine what your intentions are and how they are going to impact everything that you do.

The best thing to do when you are first beginning to set new intentions is to become mindful of all that you do in your life. Do not become overly invested in setting specific intentions with specific actions and keeping these as routine intentions. Doing so, especially in the beginning, can result in your intentions becoming a part of your autopilot. You do not want that to happen.

Since you are early on in the stages of breaking autopilot, it is better if you start setting intentions by setting them as you go. Each time you do something in your daily routine, set the intention immediately before doing it. When you awaken, shower, eat, get ready for work, drive to work, engage in your work, take your lunch break, drive home, have dinner, spend time with your family, and do anything else that comes up on your daily schedule, set the intention right before you begin. This will give you the opportunity to determine what feels right **at the moment** and how you can use this intention to shape how you will engage in the activity.

As you begin getting used to setting intentions on the go, you may find that with certain practices you begin to develop a philosophy about your intentions. Perhaps, for example, water to you is a symbol of allowing yourself to be fluid and flexible and to embrace anything that comes your way. Therefore, any time you engage with water you set the intention that it will remind you to remain fluid and flexible. These types of occurrences are natural, and you should allow them to take root when they do naturally form. As these philosophies develop, you will be able to truly formulate your own personal idea of mindfulness and how it directly nourishes your life. Mindfulness does not have to be an ever-changing thing that requires you to set new intentions every time you do something. When you do find ones that feel right, you can always set them in place and begin using them on a regular basis. The idea in the beginning is to refrain from doing this, however, until you become comfortable with truly engaging in things **without** the mindfulness becoming a part of your autopilot. Then, once you get used to these regular intention-setting practices you can begin recognizing patterns and, if it feels right, you can let certain intentions stay firmly in place in your life.

When You Outgrow Intentions

If you begin setting intentions firmly rooted in place, you may notice that over time you begin outgrowing these intentions. As we change and grow, our intentions sometimes become outdated, and they no longer serve the new aspects of ourselves that have grown into place. For this reason, it is important that you regularly check in with your intentions. This is especially true with ones that have been in place for a long time, and that may not stand out to you as much anymore.

Intentions that are no longer serving you or awakening you to the senses of life are ones that should be reassessed and changed as necessary. You are always more than welcome to change your intentions to allow them to serve you in the best way possible. You are not required to stay committed to intentions for life. These are your personal philosophies and outlooks on life, and they are more than capable of growing alongside you.

When you find that you have outgrown your intentions, simply become mindful of the times when those intentions are typically used in your life. Then, you can begin replacing them with new intentions that make you feel good. Remember, the best intention you can set is to pick the intentions that will always make you feel the best. If they are not serving you, then it is time to replace them. Outgrowing intentions is a very real thing and should be paid attention to so to avoid having your old intentions become your new autopilot.

Chapter 17: Stop Beating Yourself Up

Have you ever failed in something that you really worked for or committed something wrong towards others that put them in a very disadvantaged position? Yes, these are things that could really eat away at your inner consciousness and esteem. You will have this tendency to blame yourself and others for these things. Of course, the worst thing that could happen is when you put all the blame towards yourself that self-forgiveness is not attained at all.

Yes, there is a need for you to stop the blame game and learn to forgive. There are many reasons for you to do this. One is the fact that it is not all about you. When you beat up yourself for your mistakes and faults, your suffering is transmitted to others around you. Your co-workers, family members, and friends tend to be affected in one way or another by the pain and suffering that you are experiencing. It might not be physical in nature, but this pain and suffering that you are feeling could easily be transmitted over in the form of negativity.

Guilty feelings and the inability to forgive are also linked to health problems. This is what current researches revealed. Negative thoughts lead to the excessive release of "negative chemicals" that are pumped to all parts of the body. When you feel guilty or even angry at yourself, your blood pressure will rise, digestion will slow down, and your body will switch into a mode wherein its immunity is reduced.

Of course, there are ways through which you can stop beating yourself over mistakes and sins that you have committed. Basically, the first one is all about approaching yourself with kindness.

Don't freak out about what you did, step back, calm down, and let go of those guilty thoughts.

The next thing is about acknowledging the problem and identifying what really caused it. Admission about the presence of a problem and not just escaping away from it starts the process of self-forgiveness. You'll have to be honest and through this way, you are actually opening your mind to possible solutions on how the whole thing should never happen again.

Initiating small but relevant changes is the third one on our list. Your ability to forgive yourself can be built up by small victories that you experience on the way. As an example, you failed that big finals test and you are given a schedule for a remedial test. With the preparation you are doing for it, give yourself small quizzes that you can ace. Every time you pass those quizzes, what do you feel? Yes, your confidence level is increasing and that is the idea here!

The last thing that you'll have to work on is the right balance between expectations and the realities. Are you setting up expectations on an idealistic level? Check facts, abilities and other elements that could lead to possible results. Set your expectations based on these things. You'll find that when you are setting these things right, the odds of meeting failures in the end will be lower.

To end this chapter, it is very important to realize that you have to love yourself. There is no need to punish yourself for those things that you cannot take back. Stop the blame and move on. Whenever you are finding yourself tempted to punish yourself for mistakes and failures, just apply what you have learned on this chapter. Things will definitely be easier for you!

Chapter 18: Sitting Meditation

You have most likely seen this before – a person sitting cross-legged on a soft cushion on the floor, their eyes closed, hands resting on her knees with the palms up, with the tips of the fingers and thumbs barely touching. It is the quintessential picture of sitting meditation. It looks intriguing, romantic, ethereal, but it is actually simple when you give it a try.

Some people find the stillness boring, while others shift restlessly as they go through it, hoping that something miraculous will happen. However, what is most interesting about it is that it is merely the process of clearing one's mind from past memories and future thoughts to make way for what is happening in the present moment. There is no end goal to it. Sitting meditation is all about the journey not the destination.

Such a concept makes sitting meditation a highly attractive practice to some, and one, which is simply strange to others. It is especially strange to those who expect results to come out of dedicating one's time to it, or those who are so used to focusing on thoughts other than the present moment. Now, while there is nothing wrong with that, it is important to develop a practice of sitting meditation simply to achieve balance.

Finding the Right Sitting Position

When it comes to practicing sitting meditation, there is no "perfect" way. Traditionally, practitioners would sit on a cushion on the floor, cross their legs in one of the various positions (which you will soon learn), then proceed to meditating. Others prefer to sit in a chair with their feet flat on the ground.

To find the best sitting position for you, try out the different ways until you discover one, which makes you feel the most balanced, confident and strong. Here are some suggestions:

Sitting on a Chair

In the western world, sitting on a chair proves to be more conventional, especially if you work behind a desk. Take note of how you usually sit on a chair.

Do you sit in the right posture, in that your feet are flat on the ground and your spine is straight from your head to your hips?

Do you hunch over with your back crooked, or do you lean too far back against the chair?

If you believe your sitting posture is not right, then observe the reasons why you can't sit up straight with feet flat on the ground. It is possible that the chair is too high or too low. If so, you may use a stack of books, a stool or other such tools to place under your feet or the legs of your chair to level everything out. Once you are able to do that, you will notice that it is much easier to sit up straight.

As for your hands, you may like to place them on your knees. If you choose to let your palms face up, then it is a way to signal full acceptance. If you cause them to face down, then it is a sign of being grounded. If it is not comfortable for you to rest your hands directly on your knees or lap, then you may choose to place a cushion on your lap and place your hands on top.

Finally, notice the position of your head on your neck. Let it be naturally lifted as your straighten your spine, not letting the chin go too far down or too high up.

Close your eyes and bring your focus towards the sensations of your body as you adjust to a comfortable sitting position on your chair. After achieving the perfect balance between relaxation and confidence, you are ready to start the meditation session.

Sitting on the ground

There is something supernal about meditating on the floor, possibly because it makes one feel more grounded and connected with nature. If you prefer to do the sitting meditation in this traditional posture, you can try any one of the following positions to find one, which best fits you now.

Before starting any of them, however, always stretch and shake your legs beforehand. It is also a good idea to rotate your ankles clockwise and counter-clockwise to prepare them for the pose.

For beginners, the easiest sitting position on the ground is called the Burmese Position. This involves sitting on a cushion on the floor with one leg folded in front of the other. To try this out, choose a soft cushion to sit on, then lower yourself on it.

Once your buttocks are on the cushion and let your knees touch the ground. If your knees are too elevated and impossible to bring to contact with the ground, then you may support them with some cushions underneath.

Next, carefully bring your left heel close to your inner right thigh. They may touch, but this is not necessary. Let your right leg be in front of the left leg with its heel close to or touching your inner left thigh. Adjust the position until you feel more stable and comfortable. Straighten your spine, but not in a tense way.

Finally, place your hands on your knees or on a cushion on your lap. Ensure that the shoulders are straight but relaxed. When you are ready, you can begin with the meditation.

Whichever position you prefer, you should simply be comfortable. It is also good to remember to keep your spine straight, but not tense. By doing so, you will not only treat your body right through proper posture, but also allow it to influence your own self-confidence. Some like to imagine that by sitting up straight and tall, they become a tall and strong mountain.

How to Practice Sitting Meditation

You can practice sitting meditation anywhere and at any time during your waking hours. However, the most effective way to build it into a habit is to choose a fixed time dedicated to it. For instance, some prefer to do it first thing in the morning, right after drinking a tall glass of water to freshen up. Others like to do it at the office during their break. Some enjoy their routine of doing sitting meditation right before going to sleep.

After choosing your own special time for it, the next step is to determine the length of time you want practice it. It is highly recommended for beginners to try sitting meditation for 3 minutes and see how well they respond. After about a week or two, you may then decide to lengthen the time for a bit, say 5 minutes instead of 3 minutes. Set a timer with a soft gong or bell tone to tell you when the time you have set is up.

Finally, choose a comfortable place where nothing and no one will demand your attention during the time you have allocated for sitting meditation. In fact, it is advisable for beginners to choose a place where no one can disturb them at all.

Now, after laying all these elements out, you can follow the following steps to practice sitting meditation:

Step 1: Sit in the chair or in a cushion on the floor. Adjust until you are sitting straight but comfortably still. Start the timer.

Step 2: Relax your lids – let them droop or even close – and position your hands on your knees, lap or on a cushion on your lap.

Step 3: Adopt the intention of curiosity in the present moment. You are about to focus on it in a curious, open and non-judgmental way. You can even quietly say, "I am curious, I am open, I am meditating."

Step 4: Bring your awareness towards your breath. Notice the sensations you feel with each inhale and exhale.

Follow the path of the air as it enters your nostrils, then through your windpipes and down to your lungs. Become aware of the sensation in your chest as your rib cage expands to allow the air in.

As you exhale, notice how the air flows out from your lungs, back up through your windpipes again, and out through your nostrils.

Step 5: Continue to rest your attention on your breathing for as long as you wish.

Whenever your mind wanders off, allow the thoughts to pass you by gently. Avoid getting too involved in them. Softly guide your focus back towards your breathing.

Step 6: Let your focus expand from your breath to your body. Notice the sensations your body feels as you sit.

Become aware of the balance and stability your body has achieved. As you breathe in, notice how the air in your lungs expands your whole body, and notice the change it causes as you breathe out.

Step 7: Continue to focus on this present moment until you hear your timer go off. When it does, give yourself a minute or two to come out of the meditation gently. There is no need to rush.

Once you have read these steps, you may like to give sitting meditation a try right now. Set the timer and give it a go. After trying it, come back to this page and read on.

So, how was your experience of doing the sitting meditation? What sensations and emotions did you feel after you tried sitting meditation? Keep practicing whenever you want, because once you have conditioned your body and mind to become more open towards the stillness of the present moment, you will be more ready to add more steps and practices to your sitting meditation session. In the next chapter, you will learn how to incorporate more meditation steps moving towards deep relaxation that can be used to build upon this basic sitting meditation.

Chapter 19: What Is Meditation?

Meditation is a state of thoughtless awareness. It is not about effort or doing, rather it is simply a state of awareness. It makes sense that we would think this way because so many things in life validate the use of the mind in getting what we want. We have been raised with the belief that "if you just put your mind to it, you can do anything." There is truth to that, yet the only thing that the mind cannot "do" is meditate.

Meaning According to the Dictionary

From the Latin word Meditari, meditate technically means "to contemplate or be engaged in a reflection". It also means "to reflect or focus one's thought on something". From these definitions, it is clear then that meditation requires focus. But then again, another dictionary such as the Webster's New College Dictionary's ninth edition refers the Latin word mete as to "boundary". In its tenth edition, it mentions that the Latin word mederi means to heal or remedy and also mentions the word medesthai, meaning "to be mindful of".

At first glance, these definitions didn't really help at all. It's a bit confusing and somewhat, misleading but the meaning "to be mindful of" is by far, the closest among them. In practicing meditation, you are also training the mind to stay focused instead of letting it wander over other things. It is all about relaxing the mind, paying focus and attention and achieving a certain goal or purpose. As a beginner, this book will help you learn these basic yet, significant areas of meditation;

Meditation techniques will teach you how to take control of and connect with your mind, but the necessity of that control only pertains to the degree in which it allows you to free yourself from your mind.

Nonetheless, meditation is comprised of various mental training techniques that can help improve the physical and mental health. These techniques range from simple which you can learn by reading this book while other techniques are more complex thus, requiring the guidance of a meditation teacher.

For a more general definition, meditation simply means training your thoughts and has it stay with the present. Present moment offers true peace. Whenever you have thoughts regarding the past, there's a tendency for you to feel sudden sadness, depression and anger about the things that happened where as if you think of the future, this may lead to your anxiety and fears of what might happen. Being focused at the moment will free you from negative emotions, stress and over thinking.

Why you should meditate

When people are emotionally disturbed, angry, delusional, they may find themselves surrendering to some extremely critical physical ailments. And when they are physically not in their perfect shape, they are likely to find the world a very miserable, dull place. However, this doesn't mean that all our physical problems are caused by extreme emotional states. When you are exposed to elements to which you are or may be allergic, you tend to experience a lot of chances. These changes may include mood swings, hallucinations, depression and even physical effects. Whatever the reason, the physical ailment is usually accompanied by varied unsettling emotions.

Techniques that have been developed and used to avail the healing effects of meditation and relaxation methods have proved to be useful in limiting both the physical issues and extreme emotions that accompany them.

The aim of meditation is to overcome defilement and stray thoughts. Once you're able to control your thoughts successfully, the real state of your mind can become evident. In the absence of negative thoughts, there is no place for hatred, greed, and anger. What's more, the energy that was previously occupied by those damaging thoughts becomes available to you. This ensures your overall physical, emotional, and mental health.

Chapter 20: Letting Go

Through mindfulness we create space between our thoughts. This space gives us peace that can allow us to experience life on a deeper level. It can also allow us to be more in control of what we think. Think of your mind as a garden, and your thoughts as the seed that will either give you a lot of beautiful flowers, or nothing but weeds. Letting go through mindfulness does not mean that you do not guard your garden and control what influences you allow into your life. Neither does it mean letting things that you can control fall apart and saying "it was meant to be". No, letting go through mindfulness means that you give up the need to constantly define yourself through things or circumstances. It's about letting go of the need to define yourself through recognition from your knowledge, possessions, status, body and so on. It's about letting go for the need to compare yourself with others. Comparison is a game you can't win, so I suggest you stop it. There will always be people below you and above you in certain areas in your life. Basing your self-worth on comparison is like betting all your life savings on roulette. You'll feel good when you win but broken when you lose.

So how do we let go of these patterns? Well, it all begins with awareness. When you go about your daily life, imagine that you have camera pointed at you. This camera should not make you nervous, since the film is for your eyes only. By looking at yourself from a distance you can begin to see the moments when you define yourself through something external. Perhaps you can see where you create separation between yourself and others. It could be that you feel a strong belonging to a certain group in society. Maybe you are attached to a certain outcome and if you don't reach it, your self-worth will be affected. Jesus said that in order to find ourselves, we first have to lose ourselves. Going through a period where you're less sure of things should not scare you. Instead, it should inspire you. We all want some form of certainty, yes that's true. But our soul also craves uncertainty. The ultimate goal should therefore be to reach a state of mind of acceptance of what is. We accept both the good and the bad. We expect both, and appreciate both. We do not wish for summer when it's winter. We do not wish for day when it's night. We do not wish for better times when times are hard. Instead, we immerse ourselves in the present moment, no matter what it contains. When we reach this state of mind, we have become a warrior of peace.

Chapter 21: Conditioning + Mindfulness = Creativity.

I know we've covered a lot of ground so far. My hope is that you've not just read along but have actually tried the techniques. I know they work well with a little bit of practice, especially for those who had trouble getting a meditation practice started in the past. In this chapter, we're going to talk a bit about how to incorporate mindfulness into your everyday life and I'll end with a few thoughts on creativity and life.

There is a distinction to be made with the next bit of advice. I'm going to propose you have one goal for most of your activities. If you make "getting into the flow" your primary goal with any activity or situation in life, you will find your enjoyment of life goes up exponentially. We have already gone over how to practice getting into that state on the cushion, while walking and in everyday life. I sincerely believe if you make getting into this flow state the aim of your life, then you have the ability to turn your entire life into a mindfulness practice. Everything, good and bad, becomes more fuel for the fire of your mindfulness practice.

Conclusion

Our world is full of challenges, which may seem too complex or difficult to change. We may believe that the needed change must come from our leaders, our government, or others who hold power. The ordinary citizen may believe that there is nothing he or she can do, that the resistance to change that is posed by those in power is insurmountable.

This belief is what creates a sense of apathy or helplessness and is just another illusion created by the mind. Change starts within the individual. When the individual changes, he or she affects others, causing a Domino effect. By challenging our minds and perceptions, each of us can become a change agent. This is the purpose of mindfulness, to create a world that respects the dignity of all life.

This book offered numerous perspectives on how you can live a happier and more peaceful life. Because mindfulness practice is so drastically different from conventional thinking, many of you may find the contents of this book difficult to understand. What is important to keep in mind is that mindfulness, as with any philosophy, or way of thinking, is not the inherent answer to finding that which you desire for your life. All teachings, regardless of their teacher, or the faith that they belong to, are nothing more than signposts that are pointing to us the direction. To believe, as many people do, that the teaching itself is the answer is to say that the road sign for the Holiday Inn is the hotel itself. There is a story of a body who wanted to learn about Buddhism. He had heard that there was a very wise Buddhist monk who lived in a small hut not far from his village. The boy finds the monk who is out in his field looking at the moon. The monk called his dog, which came running to him enthusiastically. The monk pointed his finger at the moon, but the dog focused only on his finger. The monk then told the body, "Do not confuse the finger for the moon." In the same manner, do not let these teachings confuse you from what you are looking for. Instead, treat them like a guide who is giving a tour of a museum or a hiking trail; the experience you have is dependent on you, not the guide.

Thank you for reading this book on Mindfulness. I sincerely hope that it has been beneficial to you.

www.ingramcontent.com/pod-product-compliance
Lightning Source LLC
Chambersburg PA
CBHW072004070526
44583CB00015B/1322